Penguin Books
German Phrase Book
Ute Hitchin and Jill Norm...

Frau E... ...

Schreiner str. ̶8̶ 9

D 5650 Solingen 1

Herbert Müller

Ingrid

Maurerstr. 11

D 5650 Solingen 1

010-49-212 1813 14

The Penguin Phrase Books

DUTCH BY PAUL BREMAN AND JILL NORMAN
FRENCH BY HENRI ORTEU AND JILL NORMAN
GERMAN BY UTE HITCHIN AND JILL NORMAN
GREEK BY NIKOS STANGOS AND JILL NORMAN
ITALIAN BY PIETRO GIORGETTI AND JILL NORMAN
POLISH BY MAGDA HALL AND JILL NORMAN
PORTUGUESE BY ANTONIO DE FIGUEIREDO AND
JILL NORMAN
RUSSIAN BY PAMELA DAVIDSON AND JILL NORMAN
SERBO-CROAT BY JOVAN HRISTIĆ AND JILL NORMAN
SPANISH BY MARÍA VICTORIA ALVAREZ AND
JILL NORMAN

SECOND EDITION

Ute Hitchin and
Jill Norman

German Phrase Book

Penguin Books Ltd, Harmondsworth, Middlesex, England
Viking Penguin Inc., 40 West 23rd Street, New York, New York 10010, U.S.A.
Penguin Books Australia Ltd, Ringwood, Victoria, Australia
Penguin Books Canada Limited, 2801 John Street, Markham, Ontario, Canada L3R 1B4
Penguin Books (N.Z.) Ltd, 182–190 Wairau Road, Auckland 10, New Zealand

First published 1968
Reprinted 1970 (twice), 1971, 1973 (twice), 1975, 1976
Second edition 1978
Reprinted 1979, 1980, 1981, 1982, 1983, 1985, 1986

Made and printed in Great Britain by
Hazell Watson & Viney Limited,
Member of the BPCC Group,
Aylesbury, Bucks
Set in Monotype Plantin

Contents

6 Contents

8 Contents

Introduction

In this series of phrase books only those words and phrases that are essential to the traveller have been included. For easy reference the phrases are divided into sections, each dealing with a different situation.

*Some of the German phrases are marked with an asterisk – these attempt to give an indication of the kind of reply you may get to your questions and of questions you may be asked.

At the end of the book is an extensive vocabulary list and here a pronunciation guide is given for each word. In addition there is an explanation of German pronunciation at the beginning of the book and a brief survey of the essential points of grammar. It would be advisable to read these sections before starting to use the book.

For those who would like to study the phrases and perfect their pronunciation, a further aid is available in the form of two 90-minute cassettes which contain all the words and phrases spoken clearly and distinctly by German men and women.

A leaflet giving full details is available from The Institute of Tape Learning, P.O. Box 4, Hemel Hempstead, Hertfordshire (tel. 0442 68484).

Pronunciation

The pronunciation guide is intended for people with no knowledge of German. As far as possible the system is based on English pronunciation. This means that complete accuracy may sometimes be lost for the sake of simplicity, but the reader should be able to understand German pronunciation, and make himself understood, if he reads this section carefully. In addition, each word in the vocabulary is given with a pronunciation guide. Stressed syllables are printed in **bold type**.

VOWELS

German vowels are much purer than English.

Long a	as 'a' in father	symbol ah	Abend – ahbent
Short a	as 'u' in mud	symbol u	kalt – cult
au	as 'ow' in how	symbol ow	Ausland – owslunt
ä	as 'ai' in air or 'e' in bed	symbol e	Gepäck – gepeck
äu	as 'oy' in boy	symbol oy	Gebäude – geboyder
Long e	as 'e' in they	symbol ay	gegen – gaygen
Short e	as 'e' in bed	symbol e	Bett – bet

e (final)	unlike English 'e' is pronounced at the end of a word, as 'er' in sister	symbol er	Tinte – tinter
	(NB 'er': in most cases the r is more pronounced than in English)	symbol air/er	Vater – fahtair Amerika – umaireekah über – uiber
eu	as 'oy' in boy	symbol oy	Feuer – foyer
ei	as 'i' in fine	symbol ī	ein – īne leisten – līsten
i	as 'i' in bit	symbol i	Schiff – shif
i	as 'ee' in weed	symbol ee	Familie – fumeelyer
ie	as 'ee' in meet	symbol ee	Bier – beer
Long o	as 'o' in nose	symbol oh	sofort – zohfort
Short o	as 'o' in not	symbol o	von – fon
o	as 'o' in order	symbol o	Nord – nort
ö	similar to sound in 'her' and 'first' but made with the lips well rounded	symbol er	schön – shern
u	as 'oo' in good	symbol o͞o	dunkel – do͞onkell
u	as 'oo' in mood	symbol o͞o	Blut – blo͞ot
ü	similar to some Scottish pronunciations of 'u' in tone. Say 'i' as in bit with the lips rounded and pushed forward	symbol ui	Büro – buiroh

CONSONANTS

ch	rather like the sound of 'ch' in Scottish loch or the Welsh 'ch'	symbol kh	Buch – bōōkh
chs	as 'x' in six	symbol ks	Lachs – luks
d (final)	pronounced as 't'		Kind – kint
g	hard as 'g' in go, except in some endings		gut – gōōt
j	as 'y' in yacht	symbol y	ja – yah
kn	in German words which begin kn– the two sounds are pronounced separately, unlike English	symbol k-n	Knie – k-nee
qu	two sounds pronounced separately	symbol k-v	Qualität – k-vulit ayt
r	is always guttural and clearly pronounced.		
s	before a vowel is pronounced 'z' as in zoo	symbol z	Bluse – blōōzer
s	at the end of a word is pronounced 's' as in sale	symbol s/ss	Hals – huls das – duss
s	before p or t is pronounced 'sh' as in sheep	symbol sh	Stein – shtine Spiel – shpeel
sch	as 'sh' in sheep	symbol sh	Schuh – shōō
ss	often printed ß in German and pronounced as in English.		

th	as 't' in tent	symbol t	Theater – tayahtair
tz	as 'ts' in cuts	symbol ts	Netz – nets
v	as 'f' in foot or 'v' in vase	symbol f or v	viel – feel; vase – vahser
w	usually as 'v' in vase	symbol v	Wohnung – vohnōōng
x	as 'x' in wax	symbol cks	Taxi – tucksee
z	as 'ts' in bits	symbol ts	zu – tsōō

Basic grammar

There are four cases in German: NOMINATIVE (used for the subject or initiator of an action or speech), ACCUSATIVE (used for the person or thing directly affected by the action), DATIVE (used for the recipient), GENITIVE (used for the possessor). These cases are used for articles, nouns, pronouns and adjectives according to their position.

German also has three genders: masculine, feminine and neuter. They apply not only to living beings but also to inanimate objects: e.g. *der* Tisch (the table), *die* Tür (the door), *das* Bett (the bed). There are no clear rules for the use of the different genders. Similarly there are no precise easy rules on how to decline German nouns and these declensions have therefore been omitted.

DEFINITE ARTICLE

The definite article is declined as follows:

	Masculine	Feminine	Neuter	Plural for all genders	
Nom.	der	die	das	die	the
Acc.	den	die	das	die	the
Dat.	dem	der	dem	den	to the
Gen.	des	der	des	der	of the

The following words are declined in the same way as 'der, die, das':

Masculine	Feminine	Neuter	Plural for all genders	
dieser	diese	dieses	diese	this
jener	jene	jenes	jene	that
jeder	jede	jedes	jede	every, each
mancher	manche	manches	manche	many (a)
solcher	solche	solches	solche	such (a)
welcher?	welche?	welches?	welche?	which (one)?

INDEFINITE ARTICLE

The indefinite article is declined as follows:

	Masculine	Feminine	Neuter	
Nom.	ein	eine	ein	a
Acc.	einen	eine	ein	a
Dat.	einem	einer	einem	to a
Gen.	eines	einer	eines	of a

The following words are declined in the same way as 'ein, eine, ein' and, in addition, have a plural:

Masculine	Feminine	Neuter	Plural for all genders	
mein	meine	mein	meine	my
dein	deine	dein	deine	your
sein	seine	sein	seine	his, its
ihr	ihre	ihr	ihre	her, their
unser	uns(e)re	unser	uns(e)re	our
euer	eu(e)re	euer	eu(e)re	your
Ihr	Ihre	Ihr	Ihre	your
kein	keine	kein	keine	no, not a

Plural

Nom.	keine
Acc.	keine
Dat.	keine**n**
Gen.	keine**r** and, in the same way, the other words given above.

ADJECTIVES

The declension of adjectives is complex, but falls into a rigid pattern:

With the DEFINITE ARTICLE:

MASCULINE

	Singular		*Plural*
Nom.	der alt**e** Mann	the old man	die alt**en** Männer
Acc.	den alt**en** Mann	the old man	die alt**en** Männer
Dat.	dem alt**en** Mann	to the old man	den alt**en** Männer**n**
Gen.	des alt**en** Mannes	of the old man, the old man's	der alt**en** Männer

FEMININE

	Singular		*Plural*
Nom.	die jung**e** Frau	the young woman	die jung**en** Frauen
Acc.	die jung**e** Frau	the young woman	die jung**en** Frauen
Dat.	der jung**en** Frau	to the young woman	den jung**en** Frauen
Gen.	der jung**en** Frau	of the young woman, the young woman's	der jung**en** Frauen

NEUTER

	Singular		*Plural*
Nom.	das klein**e** Kind	the small child	die klein**en** Kinder
Acc.	das klein**e** Kind	the small child	die klein**en** Kinder

| Dat. | dem kleinen Kind | to the small child | den kleinen Kindern |
| Gen. | des kleinen Kindes | of the small child, the small child's | der kleinen Kinder |

With the INDEFINITE ARTICLE:

MASCULINE

Nom.	ein alter Mann	an old man
Acc.	einen alten Mann	an old man
Dat.	einem alten Mann	to an old man
Gen.	eines alten Mannes	of an old man, an old man's

FEMININE

Nom.	eine junge Frau	a young woman
Acc.	eine junge Frau	a young woman
Dat.	einer jungen Frau	to a young woman
Gen.	einer jungen Frau	of a young woman, a young woman's

NEUTER

Nom.	ein kleines Kind	a small child
Acc.	ein kleines Kind	a small child
Dat.	einem kleinen Kind	to a small child
Gen.	eines kleinen Kindes	of a small child, a small child's

Without *either* article:

MASCULINE

	Singular		*Plural*
Nom.	süsser Wein	sweet wine	süsse Weine
Acc.	süssen Wein	sweet wine	süsse Weine
Dat.	süssem Wein	to sweet wine	süssen Weinen
Gen.	süssen Weines	of sweet wine	süsser Weine

FEMININE

	Singular		*Plural*
Nom.	alte Zeitung	old newspaper	alte Zeitungen
Acc.	alte Zeitung	old newspaper	alte Zeitungen
Dat.	alter Zeitung	to old newspaper	alten Zeitungen
Gen.	alter Zeitung	of old newspaper	alter Zeitungen

NEUTER

	Singular		*Plural*
Nom.	frisches Brot	fresh bread	frische Brote
Acc.	frisches Brot	fresh bread	frische Brote
Dat.	frischem Brot	to fresh bread	frischen Broten
Gen.	frischen Brot(e)s	of fresh bread	frischer Brote

PERSONAL PRONOUNS

Nominative		*Accusative*		*Dative*		*Genitive*	
ich	I	mich	me	mir	to me	meiner	mine
du	you	dich	you	dir	to you	deiner	yours
er	he	ihn	him	ihm	to him	seiner	his
sie	she	sie	her	ihr	to her	ihrer	hers
es	it	es	it	ihm	to it	seiner	its
wir	we	uns	us	uns	to us	unser	ours
ihr	you	euch	you	euch	to you	euer	yours
sie	they	sie	them	ihnen	to them	ihrer	theirs
Sie	you	Sie	you	Ihnen	to you	Ihrer	yours

'du' (singular) and 'ihr' (plural) are the familiar address used towards friends, relatives and children.

'Sie' (singular and plural) is the formal address used towards all other people. It is written with a capital 'S' when it means 'you' and small 's' when it means 'she', or 'they'.

PREPOSITIONS

The English meanings given in the list below are often only approximations, as prepositions in German are used to indicate a number of different meanings, e.g.

Ich wohne *bei* meinen Eltern = I am living *with* my parents.

Biegen Sie rechts *bei* den Verkehrsampeln ab = Turn right *at* the traffic lights.

With the *accusative* (i.e. they always govern the noun or pronoun in the accusative case):

durch	through
für	for
gegen	against
wider	against
ohne	without
um	round, at (of time)

With the *dative*:

mit	with
zu	to
nach	to (a place), after, according to
von	of, from, by
aus	out of
bei	with, near, by
seit	since
gegenüber	opposite
ausser	except, besides

With the *accusative or dative*

in	in, into, inside
auf	on, onto

unter	under
über	over, above
an	at, on, against
vor	before, in front of
hinter	behind
zwischen	between
neben	near, beside

These prepositions are used with the *dative* when they indicate position or rest [e.g. Ich bin in dem Haus = I am in the house] or motion within a confined area [e.g. Ich gehe in dem Garten auf und ab = I am walking up and down in the garden]. They are used with the *accusative* if they indicate motion towards something or a change from one place to another [e.g. Ich gehe in das Haus = I go into the house].

With the *genitive*:

während	during
wegen	because of
trotz	in spite of
ausserhalb	outside
innerhalb	inside
statt/anstatt	instead of

INTERROGATIVE PRONOUNS

Nom.	wer?	who?	was?	what?
Acc.	wen?	whom?	was?	what?
Dat.	wem?	to whom?	wem?	to what?
Gen.	wessen?	whose?	wessen?	of what?

welcher? which? (see DEFINITE ARTICLE, p. 16)

NEGATIVES

nicht   not
nie, niemals   never

The position of these words in a sentence depends very much on the stress the speaker wants to put on them. Generally, however, they stand in front of the word or idea to be negated.

VERBS

In German, as in English, there are certain basic verbs that one uses over and over again. These are:

SEIN = to be

Present

ich bin	I am		
du bist	you are		
er	he		
sie } ist	she } is		
es	it		
wir sind	we are		
ihr seid	you are		
sie sind	they are		
Sie sind	you are		

Future

ich werde sein	I will be
du wirst sein	you will be
er	he
sie } wird sein	she } will be
es	it
wir werden sein	we will be
ihr werdet sein	you will be
sie werden sein	they will be
Sie werden sein	you will be

Perfect

ich bin gewesen	I have been
du bist gewesen	you have been
er	he
sie } ist gewesen	she } has been
es	it
wir sind gewesen	we have been

Imperfect

ich war	I was
du warst	you were
er	he
sie } war	she } was
es	it
wir waren	we were

ihr seid gewesen	you have been	ihr wart	you were
sie sind gewesen	they have been	sie waren	they were
Sie sind gewesen	you have been	Sie waren	you were

HABEN = to have

Present

ich habe	I have
du hast	you have
er	he
sie } hat	she } has
es	it
wir haben	we have
ihr habt	you have
sie haben	they have
Sie haben	you have

Future

ich werde haben	I will have
du wirst haben	you will have
er	he
sie } wird haben	she } will have
es	it
wir werden haben	we will have
ihr werdet haben	you will have
sie werden haben	they will have
Sie werden haben	you will have

Perfect

ich habe gehabt	I have had
du hast gehabt	you have had
er	he
sie } hat gehabt	she } has had
es	it
wir haben gehabt	we have had
ihr habt gehabt	you have had
sie haben gehabt	they have had
Sie haben gehabt	you have had

Imperfect

ich hatte	I had
du hattest	you had
er	he
sie } hatte	she } had
es	it
wir hatten	we had
ihr hattet	you had
sie hatten	they had
Sie hatten	you had

Most German verbs are conjugated with 'haben' [e.g. Ich habe gesehen – I have seen]. The exceptions are the verb 'sein = to be' and all verbs of *motion* which are conjugated with 'sein' [e.g. Ich bin gelaufen – I have run, Ich bin gefahren – I have travelled].

AUXILIARY VERBS

These verbs are mostly used with the infinitive of another verb, and the latter always goes to the end of the sentence.

DÜRFEN = to be permitted (may)

Present	*Imperfect*
ich darf	ich durfte
du darfst	du durftest
er ⎫ sie ⎬ darf es ⎭	er ⎫ sie ⎬ durfte es ⎭
wir dürfen	wir durften
ihr dürft	ihr durftet
sie dürfen	sie durften
Sie dürfen	Sie durften

e.g. Darf ich rauchen? = May I smoke?

KÖNNEN = to be able to (can)

Present	*Imperfect*
ich kann	ich konnte
du kannst	du konntest
er ⎫ sie ⎬ kann es ⎭	er ⎫ sie ⎬ konnte es ⎭
wir können	wir konnten
ihr könnt	ihr konntet
sie können	sie konnten
Sie können	Sie konnten

e.g. Ich kann Sie nicht verstehen = I cannot understand you.

MÖGEN = to have the inclination, liking (combined with the probability)

Present	*Imperfect*
ich mag	ich mochte
du magst	du mochtest
er	er
sie } mag	sie } mochte
es	es
wir mögen	wir mochten
ihr mögt	ihr mochtet
sie mögen	sie mochten
Sie mögen	Sie mochten

   e.g. Es mag richtig sein = It may well be right.
   Ich mag diesen Tee nicht = I don't like this tea.

SOLLEN = to have to (shall) (under order)

Present	*Imperfect*
ich soll	ich sollte
du sollst	du solltest
er	er
sie } soll	sie } sollte
es	es
wir sollen	wir sollten
ihr sollt	ihr solltet
sie sollen	sie sollten
Sie sollen	Sie sollten

   e.g. Er soll zu mir kommen = He shall come to me.

MÜSSEN = to have to (must)

Present	*Imperfect*
ich muss	ich musste
du musst	du musstest

er	er
sie } muss	sie } musste
es	es
wir müssen	wir mussten
ihr müsst	ihr musstet
sie müssen	sie mussten
Sie müssen	Sie mussten

e.g. Sie müssen um zehn Uhr hier sein = You have to be here at 10 o'clock.

WOLLEN = to want to, wish to (will)

Present	*Imperfect*
ich will	ich wollte
du willst	du wolltest
er	er
sie } will	sie } wollte
es	es
wir wollen	wir wollten
ihr wollt	ihr wolltet
sie wollen	sie wollten
Sie wollen	Sie wollten

e.g. Ich will mit dem Zug fahren = I want to go by train.

WEAK VERBS

A large group of German verbs – known as 'weak' – are conjugated by changing their endings, for instance:

MACHEN = to make, do

Present		*Future*	
ich mache	I make	Ich werde machen	I will make
du machst	you make	du wirst machen	you will make

er				he	
sie	macht	he she } makes it	er sie } wird machen es		he she } will make it
es					

wir machen — we make   wir werden machen — we will make
ihr macht — you make   ihr werdet machen — you will make
sie machen — they make   sie werden machen — they will make
Sie machen — you make   Sie werden machen — you will make

Imperfect   *Perfect*
ich machte — I made   ich habe gemacht — I have made
du machtest — you made   du hast gemacht — you have made

er   he   er   he
sie } machte   she } made   sie } hat gemacht   she } has made
es   it   es   it

wir machten — we made   wir haben gemacht — we have made
ihr machtet — you made   ihr habt gemacht — you have made
sie machten — they made   sie haben gemacht — they have made
Sie machten — you made   Sie haben gemacht — you have made

STRONG VERBS

However, many of the verbs in this phrase book can be grouped together as 'strong' verbs which means their form changes more drastically in different tenses.

SPRECHEN = to talk, speak

Present   *Future*
ich spreche — I speak   ich werde sprechen — I will speak
du sprichst — you speak   du wirst sprechen — you will speak

er		he		er		he	
sie	spri**ch**t	she	speaks	sie	wird sprechen	she	will speak
es		it		es		it	
wir spr**ech**en		we speak		wir werden sprechen		we will speak	
ihr spr**ech**t		you speak		ihr werdet sprechen		you will speak	
sie spr**ech**en		they speak		sie werden sprechen		they will speak	
Sie spr**ech**en		you speak		Sie werden sprechen		you will speak	

Imperfect

ich spr**ach**	I spoke
du spr**ach**st	you spoke

er		he	
sie	spr**ach**	she	spoke
es		it	

wir spr**ach**en	we spoke
ihr spr**ach**t	you spoke
sie spr**ach**en	they spoke
Sie spr**ach**en	you spoke

Perfect

ich habe gespr**och**en	I have spoken
du hast gesprochen	you have spoken

er		he	
sie	hat gesprochen	she	has spoken
es		it	

wir haben gesprochen	we have spoken
ihr habt gesprochen	you have spoken
sie haben gesprochen	they have spoken
Sie haben gesprochen	you have spoken

A list of the most common 'strong' verbs is given below:

Infinitive	*3rd person singular present*	*Imperfect*	*Past participle*	
beginnen	beginnt	begann	begonnen	to begin
biegen	biegt	bog	gebogen	to bend, turn
bitten	bittet	bat	gebeten	to entreat, beg (... um = ask for)
bleiben	bleibt	blieb	geblieben	to remain, stay
bringen	bringt	brachte	gebracht	to bring
denken	denkt	dachte	gedacht	to think
empfehlen	empfiehlt	empfahl	empfohlen	to recommend
essen	isst	ass	gegessen	to eat

fahren	fährt	fuhr	gefahren	to drive, travel
fangen	fängt	fing	gefangen	to catch
finden	findet	fand	gefunden	to find
fliegen	fliegt	flog	geflogen	to fly
geben	gibt	gab	gegeben	to give
gefallen	es gefällt (mir)	gefiel	gefallen	to like
gehen	geht	ging	gegangen	to go
geschehen	es geschieht	geschah	geschehen	to happen
halten	hält	hielt	gehalten	to hold
heissen	heisst	hiess	geheissen	to be called
helfen	hilft	half	geholfen	to help
kennen	kennt	kannte	gekannt	to know
kommen	kommt	kam	gekommen	to come
lassen	lässt	liess	gelassen	to leave, let
laufen	läuft	lief	gelaufen	to run
liegen	liegt	lag	gelegen	to lie
nehmen	nimmt	nahm	genommen	to take
rufen	ruft	rief	gerufen	to call
schliessen	schliesst	schloss	geschlossen	to close, shut
schreiben	schreibt	schrieb	geschrieben	to write
sehen	sieht	sah	gesehen	to see
sitzen	sitzt	sass	gesessen	to sit
sprechen	spricht	sprach	gesprochen	to speak, talk
stehen	steht	stand	gestanden	to stand
tragen	trägt	trug	getragen	to carry, wear
treffen	trifft	traf	getroffen	to meet
treten	tritt	trat	getreten	to step
trinken	trinkt	trank	getrunken	to drink
tun	tut	tat	getan	to do, make
vergessen	vergisst	vergass	vergessen	to forget
verlieren	verliert	verlor	verloren	to lose
verstehen	versteht	verstand	verstanden	to understand

| werden | wird | wurde | geworden | to become |
| wissen | weiss | wusste | gewusst | to know |

SEPARABLE VERBS

There are some verbs in German which, by having a prefix added, modify their meaning:

e.g. kommen	to come
ankommen	to arrive
fangen	to catch
anfangen	to start
fahren	to travel, drive
abfahren	to depart

When conjugated the prefix is separated from the verb in the present and imperfect and put at the end of the sentence.

e.g. abfahren: Der Zug *fährt* bald *ab* = The train leaves soon.

Essentials

First things

Yes	Ja
No	Nein
Please	Bitte
Thank you	Danke
You're welcome	Bitte sehr
No, thank you	Nein danke
Sorry	Verzeihung

Language problems

I'm English/American	Ich bin Engländer(in)/ Amerikaner(in)
Do you speak English?	Sprechen Sie Englisch?
Does anybody here speak English?	Spricht hier irgend jemand Englisch?
I don't speak (much) German	Ich spreche kein/nur wenig Deutsch
Do you understand (me)?	*Verstehen Sie (mich)?
I don't understand	Ich verstehe nicht
Would you say that again, please?	Würden Sie das bitte noch einmal sagen?
Please speak slowly	Bitte, sprechen Sie langsam
What does that mean?	Was bedeutet das?
Can you translate this for me?	Können Sie das für mich übersetzen?
Please write it down	Bitte schreiben Sie es auf
What do you call this in German?	Wie heisst das auf Deutsch?
How do you say that in German?	Wie sagt man das auf Deutsch?

Questions

Where is/are . . .?	Wo ist/sind . . .?
When?	Wann?
How?	Wie?
How much is/are . . .?	Wie teuer ist/sind . . .?/Was kostet/kosten . . .?
How far?	Wie weit?
What's that?	Was ist das?
Who is that?	Wer ist das?
What do you want?	Was wünschen Sie?
What must I do?	Was muss ich tun?
Why?	Warum?
Have you . . .?	Haben Sie . . .?
Is there . . .?	Gibt es . . .?
Have you seen . . .?	Haben Sie . . . gesehen?
May I have . . .?	Darf ich . . . haben?
I should like . . .	Ich möchte . . .
I want . . .	Ich will . . .
I don't want . . .	Ich will nicht . . .
What's the matter?	Was ist los?
Can I help you?	*Kann ich Ihnen helfen?
Can you help me?	Können Sie mir helfen?

Can you tell/give/show me?   Können Sie mir ... sagen/
                                  geben/zeigen?

Useful statements

Here is/are ...	Hier ist/sind ...
I (don't) like it	Es gefällt mir (nicht)
I (don't) know	Ich weiss (nicht)
I didn't know that ...	Ich wusste nicht dass ...
I think so	Ich glaube
I'm hungry/thirsty	Ich habe Hunger/Durst
I'm tired/ready	Ich bin müde/fertig
I'm in a hurry	Ich habe es eilig
Leave me alone	Lassen Sie mich in Ruhe
Just a minute	Einen Augenblick
This way, please	Hier entlang bitte
Take a seat	Nehmen Sie Platz
Come in!	Herein!
It's cheap	Es ist billig
It's (too) expensive	Es ist (zu) teuer
That's all	Das ist alles
You're right	Sie haben recht
You're wrong	Das stimmt nicht

Greetings

Good morning	Guten Morgen
Good day/afternoon	Guten Tag
Good evening	Guten Abend
Good night	Gute Nacht
Goodbye	Auf Wiedersehen
How are you?	Wie geht es Ihnen?
Very well, thank you	Danke, gut
See you soon/tomorrow	Bis bald/morgen
Have a good journey	Gute Reise
Have a good time	Viel Vergnügen
Good luck/all the best	Viel Glück/alles Gute

Polite phrases

Sorry	Verzeihung
Excuse me	Entschuldigen Sie bitte
Everything all right?	Alles in Ordnung?
Can't complain	Ich kann mich nicht beklagen
Don't mention it/you're welcome	Bitte sehr
Don't worry	Machen Sie sich keine Sorgen

It's a pity	(Es ist) schade
It doesn't matter	(Es) macht nichts
I beg your pardon?	Wie bitte?
Am I disturbing you?	Störe ich Sie?
I'm sorry to have troubled you	Es tut mir leid, dass ich Sie belästigt habe
Good/that's fine	Gut/das ist gut so
Thanks for your trouble	Besten Dank für Ihre Mühe

Opposites

before/after	vor/nach	for/nahkh
early/late	früh/spät	frui/shpayt
first/last	erste/letzte	airster/letster
now/later, then	jetzt/dann	yetst/dun
far/near	weit/nah	vite/nah
here/there	hier/dort	heer/dort
in/out	in/aus	in/ows
inside/outside	drinnen/draussen	**drin**nen/**drow**sen
under/over	unter/über	**öön**tair/**ui**bair
big, large/small	gross/klein	grohs/kline
deep/shallow	tief/seicht	teef/zikht

empty/full	leer/voll	layr/fol
fat/lean	fett, dick/mager	fet, dick/**mahgair**
heavy/light	schwer/leicht	shvair/līkht
high/low	hoch/niedrig	hohkh/**needrikh**
long, tall/short	lang/kurz	lung/kŏŏrts
narrow/wide	schmal/breit	shmahl/brīte
thick/thin	dick/dünn	dick/duin
least/most	mindest/meist	**min**dest/mīst
many/few	viel(e)/wenig(e)	feel/**vay**nikh
more/less	mehr/weniger	mair/**vay**nigair
much/little	viel/wenig	feel/**vay**nikh
beautiful/ugly	schön/hässlich	shern/**hes**likh
better/worse	besser/schlechter	**bes**ser/**shlekh**ter
cheap/dear	billig/euer	**bil**likh/**toy**er
clean/dirty	sauber/schmutzig	**zow**ber/**shmŏŏt**sikh
cold/hot, warm	kalt/heiss, warm	cult/his, vurm
easy/difficult	leicht/schwierig	līkht/**shvee**rikh
fresh/stale	frisch/schal, alt	frish/shahl, ult
good/bad	gut/schlecht	gŏŏt/shlekht
new, young/old	neu, jung/alt	noy, yŏŏng/ult
nice/nasty	nett/eklig	net/**ayk**likh
right/wrong	richtig/falsch	**reekh**tikh/fulsh

free/taken	frei/besetzt	frî/be**zetst**
open/closed, shut	offen/geschlossen	offen/ge**shloss**en
quick/slow	schnell/langsam	shnel/**lung**zum
quiet/noisy	ruhig/laut	roo-ikh/lowt
sharp/blunt	scharf/stumpf	shurf/shto͞ompf

Signs and public notices[1]

Achtung	caution
Aufzug	lift/elevator
Ausgang	exit
Auskunft	information
Ausverkauf	sale
Ausverkauft	sold out/house full
Bank	bank
Berühren verboten	do not touch
Besetzt	occupied/engaged
Bitte klingeln/klopfen	please ring/knock
Damen	ladies
Dolmetscher	interpreter
Drücken	push
Einbahnstrasse	one way street
Eingang	entrance

1. See also ROAD SIGNS (p. 61).

Eintritt frei	admission free
Es wird gebeten, nicht ...	you are requested not to ...
Frauen	women
Frei	free/vacant
(Fremden) führer	guide
Fussgänger	pedestrians
Gefahr	danger
Geöffnet von ... bis ...	open from ... to ...
Geschlossen	closed
Herren	gentlemen
Kasse	cash desk
Kein Eingang	no entry
Kein Trinkwasser	not for drinking
Keine Zimmer frei	no vacancies
Kein Zutritt	no entry
Männer	men
Nicht ...	do not ...
Nichtraucher	no smoking
Notausgang	emergency exit
Offen	open
Polizei	police
Post	post office
Privat	private
Rauchen verboten	no smoking

Rechts halten	keep right
Reserviert	reserved
Schlussverkauf	sale
Stehplätze	standing room
Toilette	lavatory/toilet
Trinkwasser	drinking water
Unbefugten ist das Betreten verboten	trespassers will be prosecuted
Vorsicht	caution
Warten	wait
Ziehen	pull
Zimmer frei	vacancies
Zimmer zu vermieten	room to let
Zoll	customs
Zutritt verboten	no admission

Abbreviations

ADAC	Allgemeiner Deutscher Automobil-Club	German Automobile Association
AG	Aktien-Gesellschaft	company
Bhf	Bahnhof	railway station
BRD	Bundesrepublik Deutschland	German Federal Republic

b.w.	bitte wenden	p.t.o.
DB	Deutsche Bundesbahn	German Railways
DDR	Deutsche Demokratische Republik	German Democratic Republic
d.h.	das heisst	i.e.
DIN	Deutsche Industrie-Norm	industrial standard (like B.S.)
DM	Deutschmark	German Mark
DSG	Deutsche Schlafwagen-Gesellschaft	German Sleeping Car Co.
EWG	Europäische Wirtschafts-Gemeinschaft	E.E.C.
Frl.	Fräulein	Miss
GmbH	Gesellschaft mit beschränkter Haftung	limited company
Hbf.	Hauptbahnhof	central (main) station
km	Kilometer	kilometre (8 km = 5 miles)
Lkw	Lastkraftwagen	lorry, truck
m	Meter	metre
M.E.Z.	Mitteleuropäische Zeit	Central European time
Min	Minute	minute
MWSt	Mehrwehrtsteuer	V.A.T.
nachm.	nachmittags	in the afternoon
n.Chr.	nach Christus	A.D.

ÖAMTC	Oesterreichischer Automobil- Motorrad- und Touring-Club	Austrian Automobile, Motorcycle and Touring Club
ÖBB	Oesterreichische Bundesbahnen	Austrian Federal Railways
Pf.	Pfennig	penny
Pkw	Personenkraftwagen	(private) car
Pl.	Platz	square
S-Bahn	Vorortsbahn	suburban line
SBB	Schweizerische Bundesbahnen	Swiss Federal Railways
St.	Stock	floor
Std.	Stunde	hour
Str.	Strasse	street
tägl.	täglich	daily
TCS	Touring-Club der Schweiz	Swiss Touring Club
U-Bahn	Untergrundbahn	underground
usw.	undsoweiter	etc.
v.Chr.	vor Christus	B.C.
vorm.	vormittags	in the morning
W.E.Z.	Westeuropäische Zeit	West European (Greenwich) time
z.B.	zum Beispiel	e.g.
z.Z.	zur Zeit	at present

Money[1]

Is there a bank/exchange bureau near here?	Gibt es eine Bank/Wechselstube hier in der Nähe?
Do you cash traveller's cheques?	Lösen Sie Reiseschecks ein?
Where can I cash traveller's cheques?	Wo kann ich Reiseschecks einlösen?
I want to change some English/American money	Ich möchte englisches/amerikanisches Geld einwechseln.
How much do I get for a pound/dollar?	Wieviel bekomme ich für ein englisches Pfund/einen Dollar?
Can you give me some small change?	Können Sie mir etwas Kleingeld geben?
Will you take a personal cheque?	Nehmen Sie einen Barscheck?

1. In Germany banks are open Monday to Thursday 9 a.m. to 5 p.m., Friday 9 a.m. to 4 p.m., closed Saturday.

In Austria banks are open from 8 a.m. to 12.30 p.m. and from 2.30 p.m. to 4 p.m., closed all day Saturday.

In Switzerland they are open from 8 or 8.30 a.m. to 5 p.m., closed all day Saturday.

Do you have any identification?	*Können Sie sich ausweisen?
Do you have a banker's card?	*Haben Sie eine Eurokarte?
Sign here, please	*Unterschreiben Sie hier bitte
Go to the cashier	*Gehen Sie zur Kasse
What is the current rate of exchange?	Wie ist der Wechselkurs im Augenblick?

CURRENCY

Austria: 100 Gr(oschen) = 1 S(chilling)
Germany: 100 Pf(ennige) = 1 DM (Deutschmark)
Switzerland: 100 c(entimes) = 1 F(ranc)

Travel

On arrival

Passport control	*die Passkontrolle
Your passport, please	*Ihren Pass bitte
Are you together?	*Sind Sie zusammen?
I'm travelling alone	Ich reise allein
I'm travelling with my wife/a friend	Ich reise mit meiner Frau/einem Freund
I'm here on business/on holiday	Ich bin geschäftlich hier/auf Urlaub hier
What is your address in . . .?	*Wie ist Ihre Adresse in . . .?
How long are you staying here?	*Wie lange bleiben Sie hier?
How much money have you got?	*Wieviel Geld haben Sie bei sich?
I have . . . D M/pounds/dollars	Ich habe . . . Mark/Pfund/Dollar
Customs	*der Zoll
Nothing to declare	*Zollfreie Waren

Goods to declare	*Zollpflichtige Waren
Which is your luggage?	*Welches ist Ihr Gepäck?
Do you have any more luggage?	*Haben Sie noch mehr Gepäck?
This is (all) my luggage	Das ist (all) mein Gepäck
Have you anything to declare?	*Haben Sie etwas zu verzollen?
I have only my personal things in it	Ich habe nur persönliche Sachen darin
I have a carton of cigarettes and a bottle of gin/wine	Ich habe eine Stange Zigaretten und eine Flasche Gin/Wein
Open your bag, please	*Öffnen Sie Ihre Tasche bitte
May I go through?	Kann ich durchgehen?
Where is the information bureau, please?	Wo ist die Auskunft bitte?
Porter!	Gepäckträger!
Would you take these bags to a taxi/the bus	Bringen Sie bitte diese Taschen zu einem Taxi/zum Bus
What's the price for each piece of luggage?	Wieviel verlangen Sie für jedes Gepäckstück?
I shall take this myself	Ich nehme dies selbst
That's not mine	Das gehört mir nicht
How much do I owe you?	Wieviel schulde ich Ihnen?

Signs to look for at stations, etc.

Arrivals	Ankunft
Booking Office/Tickets	Fahrkarten(schalter)
Buses	Busse
Connections	Verbindungen
Departures	Abfahrt
Exchange	Wechselstube
Gentlemen	Herren/Männer
Information	Auskunft
Ladies Room	Damen/Frauen
Left Luggage	Gepäckaufbewahrung
Lost Property	Fundbüro
Luggage lockers	Schliessfächer
Main Lines	Hauptstrecken
Non-Smoker	Nichtraucher
Platform	Gleis, Bahnsteig
Refreshments/Snack bar	Erfrischungen/Imbisstube
Reservations	Platzkarten
Smoker	Raucher
Suburban Lines	S-Bahn/Vorortsbahn
Taxi rank	Taxistand
Underground	U-Bahn
Waiting Room	Warteraum

Buying a ticket

Where's the nearest travel agency/tourist office?	Wo ist das nächste Reisebüro/ Verkehrsamt[1]?
Have you a timetable, please?	Haben Sie einen Fahrplan bitte?
What's the tourist return fare to ...?	Wieviel kostet eine Touristen-Rückfahrkarte nach ...?
How much is it first class to ...?	Wieviel kostet es erster Klasse nach ...?
A second class single to ...	Einmal zweiter Klasse nach ...
Single/one way	Einfach
A day return to ...	Eine Tagesrückfahrkarte nach ...
Is there a special rate for children?	Gibt es für Kinder Ermässigung?
How old is he/she?	*Wie alt ist er/sie?
How long is this ticket valid?	Wie lange ist diese Fahrkarte gültig?
A book of tickets, please	Ein Fahrscheinheft bitte
Is there a supplementary charge?	Muss man Zuschlag bezahlen?

---

1. Every German city has a VERKEHRSAMT. It gives information about entertainment and has a list of hotels and rooms, a HOTEL-UND ZIMMERNACHWEIS. It will recommend a hotel or guest-house, give you the price and the address, and direct you there. There is a small fee for this service.

By train and underground

RESERVATIONS AND INQUIRIES

Where's the railway station/ main station?	Wo ist der Bahnhof/ Hauptbahnhof?
Where is the ticket office?	Wo ist der Fahrkartenschalter?
Two seats on the . . . to . . .	Ich möchte zwei Plätze reservieren für den Zug um . . . nach . . .
I want to reserve a sleeper	Ich möchte einen Schlafwagen-platz reservieren
How much does a couchette cost?	Wieviel kostet ein Liegeplatz?
I want to register this luggage through to . . .	Ich möchte dieses Gepäck als Reisegepäck nach . . . aufgeben
Is it an express or a local train?[1]	Ist es ein Schnellzug oder ein Personenzug?[1]
Is there an earlier/later train?	Wann fährt der Zug davor/ danach?
Is there a restaurant car on the train?	Hat der Zug einen Speisewagen?

1. Triebwagen – railcar (used on short distances between smaller places). Personenzug – local train (stops at even the smallest station). Eilzug – stops only at bigger places (but no supplementary charge). D-Zug – stops only at main stations (supplementary charge). F-Zug – luxury train between large cities (supplementary charge). TEE – Trans-Europe-Express (first class only with special luxury features).

CHANGING

Is there a through train to . . .?

Do I have to change?

Where do I change?

When is there a connection to . . .?

Fährt ein Zug durch nach . . .?

Muss ich umsteigen?

Wo muss ich umsteigen?

Wann habe ich Anschluss nach . . .?

DEPARTURE

When does the train leave?

Which platform does the train to . . . leave from?

Is this the train for . . .?

Close the doors

Wann fährt der Zug ab?

Von welchem Bahnsteig fährt der Zug nach . . . ab?

Ist dies der Zug nach . . .?

*Türen schliessen

ARRIVAL

When does it get to . . .?

Does the train stop at . . .?

How long do we stop here?

Is the train late?

When does the train from . . . get in?

At which platform?

The train from . . . is now arriving on platform . . .

Wann kommt er in . . . an?

Hält der Zug auch in . . .?

Wie lange halten wir hier?

Hat der Zug Verspätung?

Wann fährt der Zug von . . . ein?

Auf welchem Bahnsteig?

*Der Zug von . . . hat Einfahrt auf Gleis . . .

ON THE TRAIN

We have reserved seats	Wir haben Plätze reserviert
Is this seat free?	Ist dieser Platz frei?
This seat is taken	Dieser Platz ist besetzt
Conductor	der Schaffner, die Schaffnerin
Your tickets please	*Ihre Fahrkarten bitte

By air

Where's the airline office?	Wo ist das Flugbüro?
I'd like to book two seats on the plane to ...	Ich möchte zwei Plätze buchen für das Flugzeug nach ...
Is there a flight to ...?	Gibt es einen Flug nach ...?
What is the flight number?	Wie ist die Flugnummer?
When does the plane leave/ arrive?	Wann startet/landet das Flugzeug?
When's the next plane?	Wann fliegt die nächste Maschine?
Is there a coach to the airport/ town?	Fährt ein Bus zum Flughafen/ in die Stadt?

When must I check in?	Wann muss ich mich melden?
Please cancel my reservation to . . .	Bitte machen Sie meine Flugreservierung nach . . . rückgängig
I'd like to change my reservation	Ich möchte meine Flugreservierung umbestellen

By boat

Is there a boat/(car) ferry from here to . . .?	Fährt ein Schiff/(Auto) Fähre von hier nach . . .?
How long does the boat take?	Wie lange dauert die Fahrt?
How often do the boats leave?	Wie oft fährt ein Schiff ab?
Does the boat call at . . .?	Legt das Schiff in . . . an?
When does the next boat leave?	Wann fährt das nächste Schiff ab?
Can I book a single berth cabin?	Kann ich eine Einzelkabine buchen?
How many berths are there in the cabin?	Wieviele Betten sind in der Kabine?
When must we go on board?	Wann müssen wir an Bord gehen?

When do we dock?	Wann legen wir an?
How long do we stay in port?	Wie lange bleiben wir im Hafen?

By bus, coach or tram

Where's the bus station?	Wo ist der Omnibus-Bahnhof?
Bus stop	*Bushaltestelle
Request stop	*Bedarfshaltestelle
When does the coach leave?	Wann fährt der Bus ab?
When does the coach get to . . .?	Wann kommt der Bus in . . . an?
What stops does it make?	Wo hält der Bus überall?
How long is the journey?	Wie lange dauert die Fahrt?
We want to take a coach tour round the sights	Wir möchten eine Stadtrund-fahrt machen
Is there a sightseeing tour?	Gibt es eine Stadtrundfahrt?
What is the fare?	Was kostet es?
Does the bus/coach stop at our hotel?	Hält der Bus bei unserem Hotel?
Is there an excursion to . . . tomorrow?	Fährt morgen ein Sonderbus nach . . .?
When's the next bus? . . .	Wann fährt der nächste Bus?
How often do the buses run?	Wie oft fahren die Busse?
Has the last bus gone?	Ist der letzte Bus schon weg?

Does this bus go to the town centre/beach/station?	Fährt dieser Bus in die Stadtmitte/zum Strand/zum Bahnhof?
Do you go near . . .?	Fahren Sie in die Nähe von . . .?
Where can I get a bus to . . .?	Von wo fährt ein Bus nach . . .?
Which bus goes to . . .?	Welcher Bus fährt nach . . .?
I want to go to . . .	Ich möchte nach . . . fahren
Where do I get off?	Wo muss ich aussteigen?
The tram to . . . stops over there	*Die Strassenbahn nach . . . hält dort drüben
You must take a number . . .	*Sie müssen mit der . . . fahren
You get off at the next stop	*Sie müssen an der nächsten Haltestelle aussteigen
The trams run every ten minutes/every hour	*Die Strassenbahnen fahren alle zehn Minuten/jede Stunde

By taxi

Please get me a taxi	Rufen Sie mir bitte ein Taxi
Where can I find a taxi?	Wo kann ich ein Taxi bekommen?
Are you free?	Sind Sie frei?

Please take me to the Hamburg hotel/the station/this address	Bitte fahren Sie mich zum Hotel Hamburg/zum Bahnhof/zu dieser Adresse
Can you hurry, I'm late?	Können Sie sich bitte beeilen, ich habe mich verspätet
Please wait for me	Bitte warten Sie auf mich
Stop here	Halten Sie hier
Is it far?	Ist es weit?
How much do you charge by the hour/for the day?	Wieviel verlangen Sie pro Stunde/pro Tag?
How much will you charge to take me to . . .?	Wieviel verlangen Sie für die Fahrt nach . . .?
How much is it?	Wieviel muss ich zahlen?
That's too much	Das ist zu viel

Directions

Excuse me, could you tell me . . .	Entschuldigen Sie bitte, können Sie mir sagen . . .
Where is . . .?	Wo ist . . .?
How do I get to . . .?	Wie komme ich nach . . .?
How far is it to . . .?	Wie weit ist es nach . . .?
How many kilometres?	Wieviel Kilometer?
How do we get on to the motorway to . . .?	Wie kommen wir auf die Autobahn nach . . .?
Which is the best road to . . .?	Welches ist die beste Strasse nach . . .?
Is there a scenic route to . . .?	Gibt es eine Grüne Strasse nach . . .?
Where does this road lead to?	Wohin führt diese Strasse?
Is it a good road?	Ist die Strasse gut?
Is it a motorway?	Ist es eine Autobahn?
Is there any danger of snowdrifts?	Besteht Gefahr von Schneewehen?

Will we get to ... by evening?	Werden wir bis zum Abend in ... sein?
Where are we now?	Wo sind wir jetzt?
What is the name of this place?	Wie heisst dieser Ort?
Please show me on the map	Bitte, zeigen Sie mir auf der Karte
It's that way	*Da entlang
It isn't far	*Es ist nicht weit
Follow this road for five kilometres	*Fahren Sie auf dieser Strasse fünf Kilometer
Keep straight on	*Fahren Sie geradeaus
Turn right at the crossroads	*Biegen Sie bei der Kreuzung nach rechts ab
Take the second road on the left	*Biegen Sie in die zweite Strasse links ein
Turn right at the traffic-lights	*Biegen Sie bei der Verkehrsampeln rechts ab
Turn left after the bridge	*Biegen Sie hinter der Brücke links ab
The best road is the 35	*Am besten fahren Sie die 35
Take the 35 to ... and ask again	*Fahren Sie auf der 35 bis ... und fragen Sie dann wieder

Motoring

General

Have you a road map, please?	Haben Sie bitte eine Strassenkarte?
Where is the nearest car park/garage?	Wo ist der nächste Parkplatz/die nächste Garage?
(How long) can I park here?	(Wie lange) kann ich hier parken?
May I see your licence/logbook, please?	*Kann ich bitte Ihren Führerschein/Kraftfahrzeugschein sehen?
Is this your car?	*Ist das Ihr Wagen/Auto?
How far is the next petrol station?	Wie weit ist es bis zur nächsten Tankstelle?

Car hire

Where can I hire a car?	Wo kann ich ein Auto mieten?
I want to hire a small/large car	Ich möchte einen kleinen/ grossen Wagen mieten
I need it for two days/ a week	Ich brauche ihn für zwei Tage/ eine Woche
How much is it by the hour/day/ week?	Was kostet es pro Stunde/Tag/ Woche?
Does that include mileage?	Ist Kilometergeld im Preis einbegriffen?
The charge per kilometre is . . .	*Die Gebühr pro Kilometer ist . . .
Do you want full insurance?	*Möchten Sie eine Vollkaskoversicherung?
What is the deposit?	Wieviel muss ich hinterlegen?
May I see your driving licence?	*Kann ich Ihren Führerschein sehen?
Would you sign here, please?	*Unterschreiben Sie hier, bitte
Can I return it in . . .?	Kann ich ihn in . . . zurückbringen?
Could you show me the controls/ lights, please?	Können Sie mir bitte die Schaltung/Beleuchtung zeigen?

Road signs

Ausfahrt (für Lkws)	exit (for lorries)
Bahnübergang	level crossing
Blaue Zone	restricted parking
Durchgangsverkehr	through traffic
Einbahnstrasse	one-way street
Einordnen	get in lane
Gefahr	danger
Geschwindigkeitsgrenze	speed limit
Halt!	stop!
Keine Zufahrt	no entry
Kurven	bends, curves
Langsam (fahren)	(go) slow
Lawinengefahr	avalanche area
Licht einschalten	lights on
Nicht überholen	overtaking prohibited
Parken nur mit Parkscheiben	parking discs required
Parken verboten	no parking
Rechts fahren	keep right
Scheinwerfer einschalten	headlights on
Schlechte Fahrbahn	bad surface
Seitenstreifen nicht befahrbar	soft verges
Steinschlag	falling rock

Strasse gesperrt	road blocked
Strassenbau	roadworks ahead
Strassenglätte	slippery surface
Umleitung	diversion
Verkehrsampeln	traffic lights
Vorfahrt beachten	give way
Vorsicht	caution
Zoll	customs

At the garage or petrol station

Fill it up, please	(Füllen Sie den Tank) voll, bitte
How much is petrol a litre?	Wie teuer ist das Benzin pro Liter?
... litres of standard/premium petrol, please	... Liter Normal/Super, bitte
... pounds' worth of petrol, please	Für ... Mark Benzin, bitte
Please check the oil and water	Bitte prüfen Sie das Öl und das Wasser
Could you check the brake/transmission fluid, please?	Prüfen Sie bitte die Bremsflüssigkeit/Getriebeflüssigkeit

Would you clean the windscreen, please?	Machen Sie bitte die Windschutzscheibe sauber
The oil needs changing	Das Öl muss gewechselt werden
Check the tyre pressures, please	Prüfen Sie bitte den Reifendruck
Please wash the car	Bitte waschen Sie den Wagen
Can I garage the car here?	Kann ich den Wagen hier einstellen?
What time does the garage close?	Wann wird die Garage geschlossen?
Where are the toilets?	Wo sind die Toiletten?

SELF-SERVICE PUMPS

Instructions on the pump:

1. Tankverschluss öffnen (take off petrol filler cap)
2. Münzen einwerfen (insert coins, at least 2 DM, at most 30 DM. Coins that can be used: 1 DM, 2 DM, 5 DM)
3. Zapfventil abheben (lift off nozzle)
4. Zapfen (pour in petrol)
5. Zapfventil einhängen (replace nozzle)
6. Quittung entnehmen (take out receipt)
7. Geldrückgabe (money returned, in case of fault)

Repairs, etc.

My car is broken down	Ich habe eine Autopanne
May I use your phone?	Darf ich Ihr Telefon benutzen?
Where is there a . . . agent?	Wo gibt es eine . . . Vertretung?
Have you a breakdown service?	Haben Sie einen Abschleppdienst?
Is there a mechanic?	Haben Sie einen Mechaniker?
Can you send someone to look at it/tow it away?	Können Sie jemanden schicken, der sich den Wagen ansieht/ der den Wagen abschleppt
It is an automatic and cannot be towed	Er hat ein automatisches Getriebe und kann nicht abgeschleppt werden
Where are you?	*Wo sind Sie?
Where is your car?	*Wo ist Ihr Wagen?
I am on the road from . . . to . . . near kilometre post . . .	Ich bin auf der Strasse von . . . nach . . . in der Nähe von Kilometerstein . . .
How long will you be?	Wie lange wird es dauern?
I want the car serviced	Ich möchte den Wagen überholen lassen
This tyre is flat, can you mend it?	Dieser Reifen ist platt, können Sie ihn reparieren?
The valve/radiator is leaking	Das Schlauchventil/der Kühler ist undicht

The battery is flat, it needs charging	Die Batterie ist leer, sie muss aufgeladen werden
My car won't start	Mein Wagen fährt nicht an
It's not running properly	Er läuft nicht richtig
The engine is overheating/firing badly	Der Motor läuft sich heiss/hat Fehlzündung
Can you change this faulty plug?	Können Sie diese Zündkerze auswechseln?
There's a petrol/oil leak	Ich verliere Benzin/Öl
There's a smell of petrol/rubber	Es riecht nach Benzin/Gummi
There's a rattle/squeak	Es klappert/quietscht
Something is wrong with my car/the engine/the lights/the clutch/the gearbox/the brakes/the steering	Etwas funktioniert nicht an meinem Wagen/an dem Motor/an dem Licht/an der Kupplung/am Getriebe/an der Bremse/an der Steuerung
I've got electrical/mechanical trouble	Der Wagen hat einen elektrischen/mechanischen Defekt
The carburettor needs adjusting	Der Vergaser muss eingestellt werden
I've lost my car key	Ich habe meinen Autoschlüssel verloren
Can you repair it?	Können Sie es reparieren?
How long will it take to repair?	Wie lange wird die Reparatur dauern?
What will it cost?	Wie teuer ist es?

When can I pick the car up?	Wann kann ich den Wagen abholen?
It will take two days	*Es dauert zwei Tage
We can repair it temporarily	*Wir können es vorübergehend reparieren
We haven't the right spares	*Wir haben nicht die richtigen Ersatzteile
We have to send for the spares	*Wir müssen uns die Ersatzteile schicken lassen
You will need a new ...	*Sie brauchen ein (eine, einen) neues (neue, neuen) ...
Could I have an itemized bill, please?	Geben Sie mir bitte eine Rechnung mit Einzelangaben

Parts of a car

accelerate (to)	beschleunigen	be**shloy**nigen
accelerator	das Gaspedal	**gus**pedahl
anti-freeze	der Frostschutz	**frost**shōōts
axle	die Achse	ugser
battery	die Batterie	butter**ee**
bonnet	die Motorhaube	**moh**torhowber
boot/trunk	der Gepäckraum	ge**peck**rowm
brake	die Bremse	bremser

brake lining	der Bremsbelag	**brems**belahg
breakdown	die Panne	punner
bulb	die Glühbirne	**glui**beerner
bumper	die Stoss-stange	**shtos**-shtanger
carburettor	der Vergaser	**fergah**ser
choke	die Drossel	drossel
clutch	die Kupplung	kōōplōōng
cylinder	der Zylinder	tsee**lin**der
differential gear	das Ausgleichgetriebe	owsglikhgetreeber
dip stick	der Ölmesser	**erl**messer
distilled water	das destillierte Wasser	desti**leer**ter vusser
distributor	der Verteiler	fer**tī**ler
door	die Tür	tuir
doorhandle	der Türgriff	**tuir**grif
drive (to)	fahren	fahren
dynamo	der Dynamo	dui**nah**mo
engine	der Motor	**moh**tor
exhaust	der Auspuff	**ows**pōōf
fanbelt	der Ventilatorriemen	fenteelator-reemen
(oil) filter	der (Öl) Filter	**erl**filter
foglamp	die Nebellampe	**nay**bellumper
fusebox	die Sicherungsdose	**zee**khairōōngsdohzer
gasket	der Dichtungsring	**dikh**tōōngsring
gears	die Gänge	gainger

gear-box	das Getriebe	ge**tree**ber
gear-lever	der Schalthebel	**shult**haybel
grease (to)	schmieren	sh**mee**ren
handbrake	die Handbremse	**hunt**bremser
heater	die Heizung	**hī**tsŏŏng
horn	die Hupe	**hŏŏ**per
ignition	die Zündung	**tsuin**dŏŏng
ignition key	der Zündschlüssel	**tsuind**shluisel
indicator	der Winker	**vin**ker
jack	der Wagenheber	**vah**genhayber
lights – head/side/ rear	der Scheinwerfer/das Standlicht, Parklicht/das Schlusslicht	**shīne**vairfer/ **shtunt**likht/ **purk**likht/ **shlŏŏ**slikht
lock/catch	das Schloss	shlos
mirror	der Spiegel	**shpee**gel
number plate	das Nummernschild	**nŏŏ**mernshilt
nut	die Mutter	**mŏŏ**ter
oil	das Öl	erl
petrol	das Benzin	ben**tseen**
petrol can	der Benzinkanister	ben**tseen**-cunister
propeller shaft	die Gelenkwelle	ge**lenk**-veller
piston	der Kolben	**kol**ben
plug	die Zündkerze	**tsuint**-kairtser
points	die Kontakte	kon**tuk**ter

(fuel/water) pump	die (Benzin/Wasser) Pumpe	**pōo**mper
puncture	die Reifenpanne	**rī**fenpunner
radiator	der Kühler	kuilair
reverse (to)	rückwärts fahren	**ruik**vairts fahren
reverse gear	der Rückwärtsgang	**ruik**vairtsgung
(sliding) roof	das (Schiebe) Dach	dukh
seat	der Sitz	zits
shock absorber	der Stossdämpfer	**shtohs**daimpfer
silencer	der Auspufftopf	**ows**pōoftopf
spares	die Ersatzteile	airsutstiler
(plug) spanner	der Schrauben- schlüssel	**shrow**benshluisel
speed	die Geschwindigkeit	ge**shvin**dikh-kīte
speedometer	der Zähler	tsaylair
spring	die Feder	faydair
stall (to)	stehenbleiben	**shtay**en-blīben
starter	der Anlasser, Starter	**un**lusser, shturter
steering	die Steuerung	**shtoy**erōong
steering wheel	das Steuerrad	**shtoy**er-raht
suspension	die Federung	**fay**derōong
tank	der (Benzin) tank	tunk
tappets	die Stössel	shtersel
transmission	die Kraftübertragung	**kruft**uiber-trahgōong

(spare) tyre	der (Ersatz) Reifen	(air**suts**)rīfen
valve	das Schlauchventil	**shlowkh**-fenteel
wheel	das Rad	raht
window	das Fenster	**fen**stair
windscreen	die Windschutz-scheibe	**vint**shōōts-shīber
windscreen washers	die Scheibenwasch-anlage	**shī**ben-vushunlahger
windscreen wiper	der Scheibenwischer	**shī**ben-vishair

Accommodation

Booking a room

Rooms to let/vacancies	*Zimmer zu vermieten/Zimmer frei
No vacancies	*Keine Zimmer frei
Have you a room for the night?	Haben Sie ein Zimmer für die Nacht?
Do you know another good hotel?	Kennen Sie ein anderes gutes Hotel?
I've reserved a room; my name is ...	Ich habe ein Zimmer reserviert; mein Name ist ...
I want a single room with a shower	Ich möchte ein Einzelzimmer mit Dusche
I want a room with a double bed and a bathroom	Ich möchte ein Doppelzimmer mit Bad
Have you a room with twin beds?	Haben Sie ein Zweibettzimmer?

How long will you be staying?	*Wie lange bleiben Sie?
Is it for one night only?	*Ist es nur für eine Nacht?
I want a room for two or three days/for a week/until Friday	Ich möchte ein Zimmer für zwei oder drei Tage/für eine Woche/bis Freitag
What floor is the room on?	In welchem Stock ist das Zimmer?
Is there a lift/elevator?	Gibt es einen Fahrstuhl?
Have you a room on the first floor?	Haben Sie ein Zimmer im ersten Stock?
May I see the room?	Kann ich bitte das Zimmer sehen?
I'll take this room	Ich nehme dieses Zimmer
I don't like this room	Dieses Zimmer gefällt mir nicht
Have you another one?	Haben Sie ein anderes?
I want a quiet room	Ich möchte ein ruhiges Zimmer
There's too much noise	Hier ist zu viel Lärm
I'd like a room with a balcony	Ich möchte ein Zimmer mit Balkon
Have you a room looking on to the street?	Haben Sie ein Zimmer zur Strassenseite?
Have you a room looking on to the sea?	Haben Sie ein Zimmer mit Blick auf das Meer?
Is there a telephone/radio/ television in the room?	Hat das Zimmer Telefon/Radio/ Fernsehen?

We've only a double/twin-bedded room	*Wir haben nur ein Doppel-zimmer/Zweibettzimmer
This is the only room vacant	*Dies ist das einzige freie Zimmer
We shall have another room tomorrow	*Morgen wird ein anderes Zimmer frei
The room is only available tonight	*Das Zimmer ist nur für heute Nacht frei
How much is the room per night?	Wieviel kostet das Zimmer pro Nacht?
Have you nothing cheaper?	Haben Sie nichts Billigeres?
What do we pay for the child(ren)?	Was müssen wir für das Kind (die Kinder) bezahlen?
Could you put a cot in the room?	Könnten Sie ein Kinderbett ins Zimmer stellen?
Is the service (and tax[1]) included?	Ist Bedienung (und Kurtaxe) einbegriffen?
Are meals included?	Sind die Mahlzeiten einbegriffen?
How much is the room without meals?	Wieviel kostet das Zimmer ohne Mahlzeiten?
How much is the room with full board/with breakfast only?	Wieviel kostet das Zimmer mit Vollpension/nur mit Frühstück?
Do you do bed and breakfast?	Haben Sie Zimmer mit Frühstück?
Do you have a weekly rate?	Haben Sie einen festen Preis pro Woche?

1. In health resorts only.

Would you fill in the registration form, please?	*Füllen Sie bitte dieses Anmeldeformular aus
Could I have your passport, please?	*Könnte ich bitte Ihren Pass haben?

In your room

Room service	die Zimmerbedienung
I'd like breakfast in my room, please	Ich möchte bitte Frühstück in meinem Zimmer haben
There's no ashtray in my room	In meinem Zimmer ist kein Aschenbecher
Can I have more hangers, please?	Kann ich bitte mehr Kleiderbügel haben?
Is there a point for an electric razor?	Gibt es eine Steckdose für Rasierapparate?
What's the voltage?	Wie hoch ist die Spannung?
Where is the bathroom?	Wo ist das Badezimmer?
Where is the lavatory?	Wo ist die Toilette?
Is there a shower?	Gibt es eine Dusche?
There are no towels in my room	In meinem Zimmer sind keine Handtücher
There's no soap	Es gibt keine Seife
There's no (hot) water	Es gibt kein (heisses) Wasser

There's no plug in my washbasin	In meinem Waschbecken ist kein Stöpsel
There's no toilet paper in the lavatory	In der Toilette ist kein Papier
The lavatory won't flush	Die Spülung in der Toilette funktioniert nicht
May I have the key to the bathroom, please	Kann ich bitte den Schlüssel fürs Badezimmer haben?
May I have another blanket and sheet?	Kann ich bitte noch eine Wolldecke und ein Bettlaken haben?
May I have another pillow?	Kann ich bitte noch ein Kopfkissen haben?
I can't sleep under a continental quilt	Ich kann nicht unter einem Federbett schlafen
This sheet is dirty	Dieses Bettlaken ist schmutzig
I can't open my window, please open it	Ich kann mein Fenster nicht aufmachen, bitte öffnen Sie es für mich
It's too hot/cold	Es ist zu heiss/kalt
Can the heating be turned up?	Kann die Heizung weiter aufgedreht werden?
Can the heating be turned down?	Kann die Heizung etwas mehr abgedreht werden?
Is the room air-conditioned?	Hat das Zimmer Klima-anlage?
The air conditioning doesn't work	Die Klima-anlage funktioniert nicht

Come in	Herein
Put it on the table, please	Stellen Sie es bitte auf den Tisch
I want these shoes cleaned	Lassen Sie bitte diese Schuhe putzen
I want this dress cleaned	Lassen Sie bitte dieses Kleid reinigen
I want this suit pressed	Lassen Sie bitte diesen Anzug bügeln
When will it be ready?	Wann wird er fertig sein?
It will be ready tomorrow	*Es wird morgen fertig sein

At the porter's desk

My key, please	Meinen Schlüssel bitte
Have you a map of the town/an amusement guide?	Haben Sie einen Stadtplan/ein Veranstaltungsprogramm?
Can I leave this in your safe?	Könnten Sie dies in Ihren Tresor (Safe) legen?
Are there any letters for me?	Sind Briefe für mich da?
Is there any message for me?	Ist eine Nachricht für mich da?
If anyone phones, tell them I'll be back at 6.30	Wenn jemand anruft, sagen Sie bitte, ich bin um halb sechs wieder zurück

No one telephoned	*Es hat niemand angerufen
There's a lady/gentleman to see you	*Eine Dame/ein Herr möchte Sie sprechen
Please ask her/him to come up	Bitten Sie sie/ihn heraufzukommen
I'm coming down	Ich komme hinunter
Have you any writing paper/envelopes/stamps?	Haben Sie Papier/Umschläge/Briefmarken?
Please send the chambermaid/the waiter	Schicken Sie mir bitte das Zimmermädchen/den Kellner
I need a guide/an interpreter	Ich brauche einen Fremdenführer/einen Dolmetscher
Where is the dining room?	Wo ist der Speisesaal?
What time is breakfast/lunch/dinner?	Wann wird das Frühstück/das Mittagessen/das Abendessen serviert?
Is there a garage?	Gibt es eine Garage?
Is the hotel open all night?	Ist das Hotel die ganze Nacht offen?
What time does it close?	Wann wird es abgeschlossen?
Please wake me at . . .	Bitte wecken Sie mich um . . .

Departure

I want to leave tomorrow	Ich möchte morgen abfahren
Can we check out at . . .?	Können wir um . . . abfahren?
Can you have my bill ready?	Können Sie bitte meine Rechnung fertig machen?
I shall be coming back on . . ., can I book a room for that date?	Ich komme am . . . zurück, kann ich für die Zeit ein Zimmer reservieren?
Could you have my luggage brought down?	Können Sie bitte mein Gepäck runterbringen lassen?
Please order a taxi for me	Bitte bestellen Sie mir ein Taxi
Thank you for a pleasant stay	Vielen Dank für den angenehmen Aufenthalt

Meeting people

How are you/things?	Wie geht es Ihnen?/Wie steht's?
Fine, thanks, and you?	Gut, danke, und Ihnen?
May I introduce myself?	Darf ich mich vorstellen?
My name is ...	Mein Name ist ...
This is ...	Dies ist ...
Have you met ...?	Kennen Sie ...?
Glad to meet you	Es freut mich, Sie kennenzulernen/(*more emphatic*) Angenehm
What lovely/awful weather!	Was für ein schönes/ scheussliches Wetter!
Isn't it cold/hot today?	Es ist kalt/warm heute, nicht wahr?
Do you think it's going to rain/ snow?	Meinen Sie, wir werden Regen/ Schnee bekommen?

Will it be sunny tomorrow?	Ob morgen wohl die Sonne scheinen wird?
Am I disturbing you?	Störe ich Sie?
Go away	Gehen Sie weg
Leave me alone	Lassen Sie mich in Ruhe
Sorry to have troubled you	Entschuldigen Sie die Störung
Do you live/are you staying here?	Wohnen Sie hier?
Is this your first time here?	Sind Sie zum erstenmal hier?
Do you like it here?	Gefällt es Ihnen hier?
Are you on your own?	Sind Sie allein(e)?
I am with my family/parents/a friend	Ich bin mit meiner Familie/ meinen Eltern/einem Freund (einer Freundin) hier
Where do you come from?	Woher sind Sie?
I come from . . .	Ich komme aus . . .
What do you do?	Was machen Sie beruflich?
What are you studying?	Was studieren Sie?
I'm on holiday/a business trip	Ich bin auf Urlaub/ geschäftlich hier
Would you like a cigarette?	Möchten Sie eine Zigarette?
Try one of mine	Probieren Sie eine von meinen
They're very mild/rather strong	Sie sind sehr milde/ziemlich stark

Do you have a light, please?	Haben Sie Feuer, bitte?
Do you smoke?	Rauchen Sie?
No, I don't, thanks	Nein, ich rauche nicht, danke
I have given it up	Ich habe es aufgegeben
Help yourself	Bedienen Sie sich
Can I get you a drink/another drink?	Kann ich Ihnen etwas zu trinken/noch etwas zu trinken holen?
I'd like . . . please	Ich hätte gern . . .
No thanks, I'm all right	Nein danke, ich möchte nichts

Going out

Are you waiting for someone?	Warten Sie auf jemanden?
Are you doing anything tonight/tomorrow afternoon?	Haben Sie heute Abend/morgen Nachmittag etwas vor?
Could we have coffee/a drink somewhere?	Können wir irgendwo einen Kaffee trinken/etwas trinken?
Would you go out with me?	Würden Sie mit mir ausgehen?
Shall we go to the cinema/theatre	Sollen wir ins Kino/Theater gehen?
Shall we go to the beach?	Wollen wir an den Strand fahren?
Would you like to go dancing/for a drive?	Möchten Sie tanzen gehen/ausfahren?

Do you know a good disco/restaurant?	Kennen Sie eine gute Diskothek/ein gutes Restaurant?
Can you come to dinner/for a drink?	Können Sie zum Abendessen/auf ein Gläschen zu uns kommen?
We're giving/There is a party. Would you like to come?	Wir geben/Es gibt eine Party. Möchten Sie auch kommen?
Can I bring a (girl) friend?	Kann ich einen Freund (eine Freundin) mitbringen?
Thanks for the invitation	Vielen Dank für die Einladung
Where shall we meet?	Wo sollen wir uns treffen?
What time shall I/we come?	Wann soll ich/sollen wir kommen?
I could pick you up at (time/place)	Ich könnte Sie um … von … abholen
Could you meet me at (time) outside (place)?	Könnten wir uns um … vor … treffen?
What time do you have to be back?	Wann müssen Sie wieder zurück sein?
May I see you home?	Darf ich Sie nach Hause begleiten?
Can we give you a lift home/to your hotel?	Können wir Sie nach Hause/zu Ihrem Hotel fahren?
Can I see you again?	Können wir uns wiedersehen?
Where do you live?	Wo wohnen Sie?

What is your telephone number?	Wie ist Ihre Telefonnummer?
Do you live alone?	Wohnen Sie allein(e)?
Thanks for the evening/nice time	Vielen Dank für den netten Abend/die netten Stunden
It was lovely	Es war sehr nett
Hope to see you again soon	Hoffentlich sehen wir uns bald wieder
See you soon/later/tomorrow	Bis bald/später/morgen

Restaurant

Going to a restaurant

Can you suggest a good restaurant/a cheap restaurant/a vegetarian restaurant?	Können Sie ein gutes Restaurant/ein billiges Restaurant/ein vegetarisches Restaurant vorschlagen?
I'd like to book a table for four at 1 p.m.	Ich möchte einen Tisch für vier Personen für ein Uhr bestellen
I've reserved a table; my name is ...	Ich habe einen Tisch reserviert; mein Name ist ...
We did not make a reservation	Wir haben keinen Tisch reserviert
Have you a table for three?	Haben Sie einen Tisch für drei Personen?
Is there a table on the terrace/by the window/in a corner?	Haben Sie einen Tisch auf der Terrasse/beim Fenster/in der Ecke?
This way, please	*Hier entlang bitte

We shall have a table free in half an hour	*In einer halben Stunde haben wir einen Tisch frei
We don't serve lunch until 12.30	*Das Mittagessen wird erst um halb eins serviert
We don't serve dinner until 8 p.m.	*Das Abendessen wird erst um acht Uhr serviert
We stop serving at 9 o'clock	*Wir servieren nur bis neun Uhr
Where is the cloakroom?	Wo ist die Toilette?
It is downstairs	*Die Toiletten sind unten

Ordering

Service charge	*Bedienungsgeld
Service and V.A.T. not included	*Bedienung und Mehrwehrtsteuer nicht einbegriffen
Service and V.A.T. included	*(Unsere Preise sind) Endpreise
Cover charge	*Gedeck
Waiter/waitress (*address*)	Ober/Fräulein
May I see the menu/the wine list, please?	Darf ich bitte die Speisekarte/ die Weinkarte sehen?
Is there a set menu?	Gibt es ein Tagesgedeck?
I want something light	Ich möchte eine leichte Kost
We are in a hurry	Wir haben es eilig
Do you serve snacks?	Servieren Sie einen Imbiss?

Do you have children's helpings?	Haben Sie Kinderportionen?
What is your dish of the day?	Was ist Ihre Tagesspezialität?
What do you recommend?	Was empfehlen Sie?
Can you tell me what this is?	Können Sie mir sagen, was dies ist?
What is the speciality of the restaurant/of the region?	Was ist die Spezialität dieses Restaurants/dieser Gegend?
Would you like to try ...?	*Möchten Sie ... probieren?
There's no more ...	*... sind (ist) nicht mehr da
I'd like ...	Ich möchte ...
May I have peas instead of beans?	Darf ich Erbsen statt Bohnen haben?
Is it hot or cold?	Ist es warm oder kalt?
Where are our drinks?	Wo sind unsere Getränke?
Why is the food taking so long?	Warum müssen wir so lange auf unser Essen warten?
This isn't what I ordered, I want ...	Das habe ich nicht bestellt, ich möchte ...
Without sauce/oil, please	Ohne Sauce/Öl bitte
Some more bread, please	Noch etwas Brot bitte
A little more ...	Etwas mehr ...
This is bad	Dies ist schlecht
This is uncooked/overcooked	Dies ist nicht gar/zu lange gekocht
This is stale	Dies ist alt/schal

This is too cold/salty

Dies ist zu kalt/salzig

This plate/knife/spoon/glass is not clean

Dieser Teller/dieses Messer/ dieser Löffel/dieses Glas ist nicht sauber

Paying

The bill, please

Die Rechnung bitte/Ich möchte zahlen

Does it include service?

Ist Bedienung einbegriffen?

Please check the bill; I don't think it's correct

Bitte prüfen Sie die Rechnung; ich glaube, sie stimmt nicht

What is this amount for?

Wofür ist dieser Betrag?

I didn't have soup

Ich habe keine Suppe gehabt

I had chicken not beef

Ich hatte Huhn, nicht Rindfleisch

May we have separate bills?

Können wir bitte getrennte Rechnungen haben?

Do you take credit cards/ travellers' cheques?

Nehmen Sie Kreditkarten/ Reisechecks?

Keep the change

Das ist gut so

Breakfast and tea[1]

Breakfast	Das Frühstück
A white coffee, please	Eine Tasse Milchkaffee bitte
Black coffee (with cream)	Schwarzen Kaffee (mit Sahne)
A cup of tea, please	Eine Tasse Tee bitte
I would like tea with milk/lemon	Ich möchte Tee mit Milch/mit Zitrone
May we have some sugar, please?	Können wir bitte etwas Zucker haben?
A roll and butter, please	Ein Brötchen und Butter bitte
Toast	Toast
More butter, please	Etwas mehr Butter bitte
Have you some marmalade/jam/honey?	Haben Sie Orangenmarmelade/Marmelade/Honig?
I would like a (soft/hard) boiled egg	Ich möchte ein (weich/hart) gekochtes Ei
Ham	der Schinken
Cheese	der Käse
What fruit juices have you?	Was für Obstsäfte haben Sie?
Orange/tomato/(black, red) currant juice	der Apfelsinensaft (Orangensaft)/Tomatensaft/Johannisbeersaft (schwarz, rot)

1. Don't forget to go into a 'Cafe' or 'Konditorei', particularly in Austria. To try one of the wide selection of 'Torten', a pastry speciality, with names like Sachertorte, Kaffeecremetorte, Linzertorte, Imperialtorte, will be an experience for any foreign visitor.

Yoghurt	der Joghurt
Pastry[1]	das Gebäck
Flaky/short pastry	der Blätterteig/Mürbeteig
Tart/Layer cake	die Torte
Cake	der Kuchen

Snacks and picnics

Can I have a sandwich, please?	Kann ich bitte ein belegtes Brot haben?
What are those things over there?	Was ist das dort?
What are they made of?	Woraus ist es gemacht?
What is in them?	Was ist da drin?
I'll have one of these, please	Eins davon bitte
Beefburger	die Frikadelle
Biscuits	die Kekse
Bread	das Brot
Butter	die Butter
Cheese	der Käse
Chips	die Pommes frites
Chocolate bar	die Tafel Schokolade

1. For names of cakes and pastry see pp.103–5.

Egg(s)	das Ei (die Eier)
Ham	der Schinken
Ice cream (*flavours: page* 103)	das Eis
Pancakes	der Pfannkuchen, die Palatschinke
Pickles	die Essigfrüchte
Meat/fruit pie	die Fleischpastete/Fruchttorte
Roll	das Brötchen
Salad	der Salat
Sausage (roll)	die Wurst(pastete)
Snack	der Imbiss
Snack bar	der Schnellimbiss
Soup	die Suppe
Tomato	die Tomate
Waffles	die Waffel

Drinks[1]

Bar	die Bar, die Schenke, der Ausschank
Café	das Café, das Kaffeehaus
What will you have to drink?	Was möchten Sie trinken?

1. For the names of beverages see pp. 106–8.

A bottle of the local wine, please	Eine Flasche hiesigen Wein bitte
I want to see the wine list	Ich möchte die Weinkarte sehen
Do you serve wine by the glass?	Haben Sie offenen Wein?
Carafe/glass	die Karaffe/das Glas[1]
Bottle/half bottle	die Flasche/kleine Flasche
Two glasses of beer, please	Zwei Gläser Bier bitte
Pint/half pint	ein grosses/kleines Bier
Do you have draught beer?	Haben Sie Bier vom Fass?
Light/dark beer	Helles/dunkles Bier
Two more beers	Noch zwei Bier
Neat/on the rocks	Pur/mit Eis
With (soda) water	mit (Soda) Wasser
Mineral water (with/without gas)	Mineralwasser (mit/ohne Kohlensäure)
Ice cubes	die Eiswürfel
Cheers!	Prost!
I'd like a glass of water, please	Ich möchte bitte ein Glas Wasser
The same again, please	Noch einmal dasselbe bitte
Three black coffees and one with cream	Dreimal schwarzen Kaffee und einen mit Sahne
Tea with milk/lemon	Tee mit Milch/Zitrone

1. Usually open wine is sold by the 'Viertel', a glass holding a quarter litre i.e. a third of a standard bottle or two of our standard glasses.

May we have an ashtray?   Können wir einen Aschenbecher
                                 haben?

Restaurant vocabulary

ashtray	der Aschenbecher	**ush**en-bekher
bill	die Rechnung	**rekh**nŏŏng
bowl	die Schüssel	**shui**sel
bread	das Brot	broht
butter	die Butter	**bŏŏ**ter
cigarettes	die Zigaretten	tseegu**ret**ten
cloakroom	die Toilette	twu**let**ter
course (dish)	der Gang	gung
cream	die Sahne	**zah**ner
cup	die Tasse	**tuss**er
dressing	die Salatsosse	zu**laht**-sohser
fork	die Gabel	**gah**bel
glass	das Glas	glus
headwaiter	der Oberkellner	**oh**berkelnair
hungry (to be)	Hunger haben, hungrig sein	**hŏŏn**gair hahben, **hŏŏn**grikh zīne
knife	das Messer	**mess**er
light (easily digested) meals	die Schonkost	**shohn**kost

matches	die Streichhölzer	**shtrīkh**-herltser
menu	die Speisekarte	**shpī**zerkurter
mustard	der Senf	zenf
napkin	die Serviette	zairvee**yet**ter
oil	das Öl	erl
pepper	der Pfeffer	pfeffer
pickles	die Essigfrüchte	es**ī**khfruikhter
plate	der Teller	tellair
restaurant	das Restaurant	resto**runt**
salt	das Salz	sults
sauce	die Sauce	sohser
saucer	die Untertasse	ŏŏntair-tasser
service	die Bedienung	be**deen**ŏŏng
spoon	der Löffel	**lerf**fel
sugar	der Zucker	ts**ŏŏ**ker
table	der Tisch	tish
tablecloth	das Tischtuch	**tish**tŏŏkh
thirsty (to be)	Durst haben, durstig sein	dŏŏrst hahben, **dŏŏr**stikh zīne
tip	das Trinkgeld	**trink**gelt
toothpick	der Zahnstocher	**tsahn**-shtokhair
vegetarian	der Vegetarier	fege**tah**ree-er
vinegar	der Essig	es**ī**kh
waiter	der Kellner	**kel**nair

| waitress | die Kellnerin | **kel**nairin |
| water | das Wasser | **vu**ssair |

The menu

VORSPEISEN	HORS D'ŒUVRES
Artischocken	artichokes
Austern	oysters
Gänseleberpastete	pâté de foie
Geräucherter Lachs	smoked salmon
Königinpastete	pastry filled with *ragoût fin*
Matjesfilet ('Hausfrauenart')	herring fillet (with apple and sour cream)
(Geeiste) Melone	(iced) melon
Ölsardinen (mit Brot)	tinned sardines (with bread)
Räucheraal	smoked eel
Rollmops	rollmops
Russische Eier	hard boiled eggs with caviare, capers and mayonnaise
(Westfälischer) Schinken	(raw) ham
Schinkenwurst	ham sausage
(Weinberg)schnecken	snails
Spargelspitzen	asparagus tips

Stangenspargel mit Kräutersauce	asparagus with herb sauce
Strammer Max	ryebread, raw ham and fried egg
Wurstplatte	assorted sliced sausage

SUPPEN	SOUPS
Aalsuppe	eel soup
Bohnensuppe	bean soup
Erbsensuppe	pea soup
Gaisburger Marsch	vegetable soup with dumplings
Gemüsesuppe	vegetable soup (minestrone)
Gulaschsuppe	beef and paprika soup
Hühnerbrühe	chicken broth
Kartoffelsuppe	potato soup
Kirschkaltschale	cold cherry soup
Kraftbrühe mit Ei/Magen	bouillon with egg/tripe
Leberknödelsuppe	clear soup with liver dumplings
Linsensuppe	lentil soup
Mandelsuppe	almond and cream soup
Nudelsuppe	noodle soup
Ochsenschwanzsuppe	oxtail soup
Schildkrötensuppe	turtle soup
Tomatensuppe	tomato soup

Zwiebelsuppe — onion soup

FISCH / FISH

Aal	eel
Aal grün mit Dillsauce	fresh eel with dill sauce
Austern	oysters
Barsch	perch
Forelle	trout
Garnele	shrimp
Hecht	pike
Heilbutt	halibut
Hering	herring
Hummer	lobster
Kabeljau	cod
Karpfen	carp
Krabben	small shrimps
Krebs	crab
Lachs, Salm	salmon
Makrele	mackerel
Muscheln	mussels
Rotbarsch	redfish
Sardellen	anchovies
Schellfisch	haddock
Scholle	plaice

Seebarsch	bass
Seezunge	sole
Steinbutt	turbot
Thunfisch	tunny
Zander	pike-perch

FLEISCH — MEAT

Lamm/Hammel: — lamb/mutton:
  Hammelbraten/Lammbraten — roast mutton/lamb
  Lammskeule — roast leg of lamb
  Hammelragout — mutton stew

Kalb: — veal:
  Kalbsbrust — breast of veal
  Kalbshaxe — roast knuckle of veal
  Kalbskoteletts — veal cutlets, chops
  Kalbsvögel — veal roulade
  (Wiener) Schnitzel — (fried) escalope of veal

Rind: — beef:
  Beefsteak — steak
  Deutsches Beefsteak — minced beef, hamburger
  gekochte Rinderbrust — boiled brisket of beef
  Gulasch — goulash
  Rinderbraten — roast beef
  Rinderfilet — fillet of beef
  Rindsrouladen — stuffed beef
  Rinderschmorbraten — braised beef
  Sauerbraten — braised pickled beef
  Stroganoff — goulash of choice meat

Schweinefleisch:	pork:
(Kasseler) Rippchen	(smoked) pork chop
Schweinebraten	roast pork
Schweinefilet	loin of pork
Eisbein	pickled pork knuckle
Spanferkel	sucking pig

WÜRSTE UND INNEREIEN	SAUSAGES AND OFFAL
Blutwurst	black pudding
Bratwurst	frying sausage
Knackwurst	frankfurter
Kochwurst	cold cuts
Nürnberger Würstchen	small spiced chipolatas
Pinkel	smoked sausage with onions
Weisswurst	veal sausage
Flecke	tripe
Fleischkloss	meatball
Frikadelle	rissole, croquette
Hirn	brain
Kalbsbries (*North German:* Kalbsmilcher)	sweetbreads
Leber	liver
Nieren	kidneys
Ochsenschwanz	oxtail

Schinken	ham (smoked raw)
gekochter Schinken	cooked ham
Schlachtplatte	mixed cold meat
Speck	bacon
Zunge	tongue

WILD UND GEFLÜGEL	GAME AND POULTRY
Ente	duck
Fasan	pheasant
Gans	goose
Hähnchen/Huhn	chicken
am Spiess	roast
Flügel	wing
Brust	breast
Hase	hare
Hasenpfeffer	jugged hare
(gespickter) Hirsch	(larded) deer
Huhn	chicken
Kaninchen	rabbit
Rebhuhn	partridge
Reh(braten)	(roast) venison
Rehrücken	saddle of deer
Taube	pigeon
Truthahn, Pute	turkey

GEMÜSE UND SALAT	VEGETABLES AND SALAD
Blumenkohl	cauliflower
Bohnen	beans
grüne Bohnen	green beans
Stangenbohnen	runner beans
weisse Bohnen	haricot beans
Brunnenkresse	watercress
Champignons	mushrooms
Edelpilze	(best varieties of wild) mushrooms
Erbsen	peas
Grüner Salat	lettuce
Grünkohl	kale
Gurke	cucumber
Gewürzgurken	pickled cucumbers
Himmel und Erde	potato and apple
Kartoffeln	potatoes
Salzkartoffeln	boiled potatoes
Kartoffelpüree	mashed potatoes
Kartoffelklösse	potato dumplings
Pommes frites	chips
Bratkartoffeln	fried potatoes
Rösti	hashed brown potatoes
Kartoffelsalat	potato salad
Kastanien	chestnuts
Knoblauch	garlic

Kohl (Weiss-, Rot-)	cabbage (white, red)
Kopfsalat	(cabbage) lettuce
Kürbis	pumpkin, marrow
Lauch, Porree	leeks
Meerrettich	horse radish
Paprika (-schoten)	peppers
Pfifferlinge	mushrooms (chanterelle)
Pilze	mushrooms
Reis	rice
Rettich	radish
Rosenkohl	brussels sprouts
Rote Beete	beetroots
Rüben	swedes
Salat	lettuce/salad
Sauerkraut	pickled cabbage
Schwarzwurzeln	scorzonera
Sellerie	celery
Spargel	asparagus
Spinat	spinach
Steinpilze	mushrooms (Boletus edulis, cèpe)
Tomaten	tomatoes
Weisse Rübe	turnip
Wirsingkohl	savoy cabbage

Wurzeln (Möhren, Karotten)	carrots
Zwiebeln	onions

KNÖDEL

DUMPLINGS AND NOODLES

Leberknödeln	liver dumplings
Kartoffelknödeln	potato dumplings
Klösse	dumplings
Kräuterklösse	herb dumplings
Maultasche	Swabian ravioli
Nockerl	dumpling
Nudeln	noodles
Spätzle	German variety of pasta

EIER

EGGS

gekochtes Ei (weich, hart)	boiled egg (soft, hard)
Omelett	omelette
mit Pilzen	with mushrooms
mit Kräutern	with herbs
Bauernomelett	with diced bacon and onion
Rührei	scrambled eggs
Russische Eier	hard boiled eggs with caviare, capers and mayonnaise
Spiegeleier	fried eggs
verlorene Eier	poached eggs

KÄSE	CHEESE
Allgäuer, Emmentaler	Swiss cheese
Käseteller	cheese board
Kümmelkäse	cheese with caraway seed
Rahmkäse, Sahnekäse	cream cheese
Räucherkäse	smoked cheese
Schmelzkäse	cheese spread
Thüringer Käse, Harzkäse	sausage-shaped cheeses made from curd

NACHSPEISEN UND KUCHEN	DESSERTS AND CAKES
Apfelkuchen	apple cake
Apfelstrudel	flaky pastry stuffed with apple, walnut, spices
Auflauf	soufflé
Eis (Speiseeis):	ice cream:
Erdbeer-	strawberry
gemischtes-	mixed
Mokka-	coffee
Nuss-	nut
Schokoladen-	chocolate
Vanille-	vanilla
Eisbecher	ice cream with fresh fruit
Frisches Obst	fresh fruit
Frucht Törtchen	small fruit tart

Kaiserschmarren	shredded pancake with raisins and syrup
Käsetorte	cheesecake
Keks	biscuit
Krapfen	doughnuts
Kuchen	cake
Lebkuchen	spiced cake, gingerbread
Linzer Torte	cake spread with jam, topped with whipped cream
Makronen	macaroons
Mohrenkopf	pastry filled with cream, topped with chocolate
Mokka Torte	coffee cake
Nusstorte	nut cake
Obstkompott	stewed fruit
Obstkuchen	fruit tart
Obstsalat	fruit salad
Palatschinke	pancake filled either with sausage or with cheese and nuts or with jam
Pfannkuchen	pancakes, doughnuts, fritters
Pfirsich Melba	peach melba
Pflaumenkuchen	plum cake
rote Grütze	raspberries or redcurrants cooked with semolina, served with cream

Sacher Torte	chocolate cake spread with jam and chocolate icing
Sandtorte	Madeira cake
Schlagsahne	whipped cream
Stollen	rich cake with fruit and nuts
Streuselkuchen	cake sprinkled with almonds and cinnamon butter
Torte	tart, flat cake

OBST UND NÜSSE — FRUIT AND NUTS

Ananas	pineapple
Apfel	apple
Apfelsine	orange
Aprikose	apricot
Banane	banana
Birne	pear
Brombeere	blackberry
Erdbeere	strawberry
Feige	fig
Haselnuss	hazelnut
Himbeere	raspberry
Johannisbeere (rot)	red currant
Johannisbeere (schwarz)	blackcurrant
Kirsch	cherry

Mandarine	mandarin orange, tangerine
Mandel	almond
Melone	melon
Pampelmuse	grapefruit
Pfirsich	peach
Pflaume	plum
Reineclaude	greengage
Stachelbeere	gooseberry
(Wein)traube	grape
Walnuss	walnut
Wassermelone	water melon
Zitrone	lemon
Zwetschen	plums

GETRÄNKE	DRINKS
Alkohol	alcohol
Apfelsaft	applejuice
Apfelsinensaft	orange juice
Apfelwein	cider
Bier (hell/dunkel)	beer (light/dark)
Bockbier	bock beer (dark and very strong)
Bowle	fruit cup
Cognac	brandy
(Himbeer)geist	(raspberry) brandy

Glühwein	mulled wine
Grog	grog
Kaffee	coffee
Milchkaffee	white
Schwarzer	black
mit Sahne	with cream
Kaffee Haag (ohne Caffein)	(caffeine free)
Likör	liqueur
Limonade	lemonade
Märzen	strong beer
Milch	milk
Mineralwasser	mineral water
Obstsaft	fruit juice
Orangeade	orangeade
Pilsener	lager
Portwein	port
Rum	rum
Sekt	a German sparkling wine
Schnaps	a German grain spirit
Sherry	sherry
Sodawasser	soda water
Tee	tea
Wasser	water
(Kirsch-/Zwetschen) wasser	(cherry/plum) brandy

Wein	wine
offen	open, by the glass
rot	red
weiss	white
süss	sweet
trocken	dry
Weinbrand	brandy
Wermut	vermouth
Whisky	whisky

SOME COOKING METHODS AND SAUCES

fleisch – rot	meat – rare
halbdurch	medium
durchgebraten	well-done
blau	au bleu
gebacken	baked
gebraten	roast
(in der Pfanne) gebraten	fried
gedämpft	steamed, stewed
gefüllt	stuffed
gegrillt	grilled
gekocht	boiled
geräuchert	smoked
gerieben	grated
geschmort	braised, stewed
geschwenkt	sautéed

mariniert	marinated
... püree	creamed ...
roh	raw
Butter-	buttered ...
Grüne Sauce	mayonnaise (or vinaigrette with chopped egg) with mixed green herbs
Holländisch	with mayonnaise
Holstein	topped with fried egg, garnished with anchovy (the grand version with assorted seafood)
nach Jägerart	sautéed with mushrooms, in wine sauce
Kräuter(butter)	herb (butter)
Petersilien-	parsleyed ...
Sahne-/Rahm-	... and cream
Senf-	mustard ...
Sülz-	... in aspic

Shopping[1] and services

Where to go

Which is the best . . . ?	Welches ist der/die/das beste . . . ?
Where is the nearest . . . ?	Wo ist der/die/das nächste . . . ?
Can you recommend a . . . ?	Können Sie einen/eine/ein . . . empfehlen?
Where is the market?	Wo ist der Markt?
Is there a market every day?	Ist jeden Tag Markt?
Where can I buy . . .	Wo kann ich . . . kaufen?
When are the shops open?	Wann sind die Geschäfte geöffnet?

1. Shopping hours in Germany vary in different parts of the country; generally however shops open at 9 a.m. and close at 6.30 p.m. They are closed on Sundays and public holidays (p. 165) and on Saturday afternoons. In Austria most shops are open from 8 a.m. to 12 noon and from 2 to 6 p.m. and are closed either Wednesday or Saturda afternoon. In Switzerland shops are open from 8 a.m. to 12 noon and from 2 to 6 p.m., closed Saturday afternoons.

antique shop	der Antiquitätenladen	unteekveetayten-lahden
baker	der Backer/die Bäckerei	**buck**er/becker**ī**
barber (see p. 123)	der Friseur	free**zer**
bookshop	die Buchhandlung	**bōōkh**-huntlōōng
butcher (see pp. 97 and 98)	die Metzgerei/die Schlachterei	metsge**rī/shlukh**ter**ī**
chemist (see p. 117)	die Apotheke (*for medicines*)/die Drogerie (*for cosmetics, etc.*)	upoh**tay**-ker/droh-gair-**ee**
confectioner (see p. 103)	die Konditorei	condeeto**rī**
department store (see pp. 114 and 119)	das Warenhaus	**vah**renhows
dry cleaner (see p. 125)	die (chemische) Reinigung	(**kay**misher) **ry**nigōōng
fishmonger (see p. 96)	die Fischhandlung	**fish**-huntlōōng
florist	das Blumengeschäft	**blōō**men-gesheft
greengrocer (see pp. 100 and 105)	die Gemüsehandlung	ge**muise**-huntlōōng
grocer (see p. 122)	das Lebensmittel-geschäft	**lay**bensmittel-gesheft
hairdresser (see p. 123)	der (Damen)friseur	(**dahmen**)free**zer**

hardware store (see p. 124)	die Eisenwaren-handlung	**ī**senvahren-huntlŏŏng
jeweller (see p. 131)	der Juwelier	yŏŏve**leer**
launderette	die Schnellwä-scherei	**shnel**-vesherī
laundry (see p. 125)	die Wäscherei	vesherī
liquor/wine store (see p. 106)	die Spirituosen-/Weinhandlung	spee-ree-tŏŏ-**oh**-zen-/**vīne**-huntlŏŏng
newsagent (see p. 126)	die Zeitungshandlung	tsytŏŏngs-huntlŏŏng
optician (see p. 130)	der Optiker	**opt**eekair
shoemaker	der Schuhster	shŏŏ-stair
shoe shop (see p. 119)	das Schuhgeschäft	**shŏŏ**-gesheft
sports shop	das Sportgeschäft	**shport**-gesheft
stationer (see p. 127)	das Schreibwaren-geschäft	**shrīp**vahren-gesheft
supermarket	der Supermarkt	**zuper**-murkt
tobacconist (see p. 129)	der Tabakladen	**tu**buck-lahden
toy shop	das Spielwaren-geschäft	**shpeel**vahren-gesheft

In the shop

Self service	*Selbstbedienung
Sale (clearance)	*Schlussverkauf/Ausverkauf
Cash desk	*Kasse
Shop assistant	Der Verkäufer/die Verkäuferin
Manager	Der Geschäftsführer
Can I help you?	*Was darf es sein?
I want to buy ...	Ich möchte ... kaufen
Do you sell ...?	Verkaufen Sie ...?
I'm just looking round	Ich möchte mich nur umsehen
I don't want to buy anything now	Ich möchte im Augenblick nichts kaufen
Could you show me ...?	Könnten Sie mir bitte ... zeigen?
We do not have that	*Das haben wir leider nicht
You'll find them at that counter	*Sie sind dort auf dem Verkaufstisch
We've sold out but we'll have more tomorrow	*Wir sind im Augenblick ausverkauft, aber morgen haben wir mehr
Anything else?	*Sonst noch etwas?
That will be all	Das ist alles
Will you take it with you?	*Möchten Sie es mitnehmen?
I will take it with me	Ich nehme es gleich mit

Please send it to this address/X hotel

Bitte schicken Sie es an diese Adresse/ins Hotel X

Choosing

I want something in leather/green	Ich möchte etwas aus Leder/in grün
I need it to match this	Es soll hierzu passen
I like the one in the window	Das im Fenster gefällt mir
Could I see that one, please?	Darf ich das mal sehen, bitte?
I like the colour but not the style	Mir gefällt die Farbe, aber nicht der Schnitt
I want a darker/lighter shade	Ich möchte einen dunkleren/helleren Farbton
I need something warmer/thinner	Ich brauche etwas Wärmeres/Dünneres
Do you have one in another colour/size?	Haben Sie es in einer anderen Farbe/Grösse?
Have you anything better/cheaper?	Haben Sie etwas Besseres/Billigeres?
How much is this?	Was kostet das?
That is too much for me	Das ist mir zu teuer
What's it made of?	Woraus ist es gemacht?
What size is this?	Welche Grösse ist das?

I take size[1] ...

The English/American size is ...

My collar/chest/waist is ...

Can I try it on?

It's too short/long/tight/loose

Have you a larger one/smaller one?

Ich brauche Grösse ...

Die englische/amerikanische Grösse ist ...

Meine Kragenweite/mein Brustumfang/meine Taillenweite ist ...

Kann ich es anprobieren?

Es ist zu kurz/lang/eng/weit

Haben Sie ein grösseres/ kleineres

Colours

beige	beige	behj
black	schwarz	shvurts
blue	blau	blow
brown	braun	brown
gold	golden	gohlden
green	grün	gruin
grey	grau	grow
mauve	lila	leelah
orange	orangenfarbig	orunjenfurbikh
pink	rosa	rozah

1. See table (p. 120) for continental sizes.

purple	purpur	**pŏŏr**pŏŏr
red	rot	roht
silver	silbern	**zil**bairn
white	weiss	vis
yellow	gelb	gelp

Complaints

I want to see the manager	Ich möchte den Geschäftsführer sprechen
I bought this yesterday	Ich habe dies gestern gekauft
It doesn't work/fit	Es funktioniert/passt nicht
This is dirty/torn/broken/bad	Es ist schmutzig/zerrissen/kaputt/schlecht
This is stained/cracked	Es hat Flecken/einen Sprung
Will you change it please?	Können Sie es bitte umtauschen?
Will you refund my money?	Können Sie mir bitte mein Geld zurückgeben?
Here is the receipt	Hier ist die Quittung

Paying

How much is this?	Wie teuer ist das?
That's 10 DM, please	*Das macht zehn Mark bitte
They are one mark each	*Sie kosten eine Mark pro Stück
How much does that come to?	Was macht das?
That will be . . .	*Das macht . . .
Can I pay with English/American currency?	Nehmen Sie englisches/ amerikanisches Geld?
Do you take credit cards/ traveller's cheques?	Nehmen Sie Kreditkarten/ Reiseschecks?
Please pay the cashier	*Bitte, zahlen Sie an der Kasse
May I have a receipt, please	Kann ich bitte eine Quittung haben?
You've given me too little/too much change	Sie haben mir zu wenig/zu viel Geld herausgegeben

Chemist[1]

Can you prepare this prescription for me, please?	Können Sie bitte dieses Rezept für mich zubereiten?
Have you a small first-aid kit?	Haben Sie einen kleinen Verbandkasten?
I want some aspirin/sun cream (for children)	Ich möchte Aspirin/ Sonnencreme (für Kinder)

1. You go to an Apotheke for prescriptions, medicines, etc., and to a Drogerie for toilet requisites.

A tin of adhesive plaster	Eine Schachtel Hansaplast/ Heftpflaster
Can you suggest something for indigestion/constipation/ diarrhoea?	Können Sie etwas vorschlagen gegen Verdauungsstörung/ Verstopfung/Durchfall
I want something for insect bites	Ich möchte etwas gegen Insektenstiche
Can you give me something for sunburn?	Können Sie mir etwas gegen Sonnenbrand geben?
I want some throat lozenges/ stomach pills/antiseptic cream/ lipsalve	Ich brauche Halspastillen/ Magentabletten/ antiseptische Creme/ Lippensalbe
Do you have sanitary towels/ tampons/cotton wool?	Haben Sie Binden/Tampons/ Watte?
I need something for insect bites/ a hangover/travel sickness	Ich brauche etwas für Insektenstiche/einen Kater/ Reiseübelkeit

Toilet requisites[1]

A packet of razor blades, please	Eine Schachtel Rasierklingen bitte
How much is this after-shave lotion?	Wie teuer ist dieses Rasierwasser?
A tube of toothpaste, please	Eine Tube Zahnpasta bitte

1. You go to an Apotheke for prescriptions, medicines, etc., and to a Drogerie for toilet requisites.

A box of paper handkerchiefs/a roll of toilet paper, please

Eine Schachtel Papiertaschentücher/eine Rolle Toilettenpapier, bitte

I want some eau-de-cologne/ perfume/cream

Ich möchte Kölnisch Wasser/ Parfüm/Creme

May I try it?

Kann ich es ausprobieren?

What kinds of soap have you?

Welche Arten von Seife haben Sie?

A bottle/tube of shampoo, please, for dry/greasy hair

Eine Flasche/Tube Schampoo bitte für trockenes/fettiges Haar

Do you have any suntan oil/ cream?

Haben Sie Sonnenöl/ Sonnencreme?

Clothes and shoes[1]

I want a hat/sunhat

Ich möchte einen Hut/ Sonnenhut

Can I see some dresses, please?

Kann ich mir bitte einige Kleider ansehen?

Where is the underwear/ haberdashery/coats department?

Wo ist die Unterwäsche-/ Kurzwaren-/Mantel- abteilung?

Where are beach clothes?

Wo finde ich Strandkleidung?

1. For sizes see p. 120.

I want a short/long sleeved shirt, collar size ...	Ich möchte ein Hemd mit kurzen/langen Ärmeln, Kragenweite ...
Where can I find socks/stockings?	Wo finde ich Socken/Strümpfe?
I am looking for a blouse/bra/dress/jumper	Ich suche eine Bluse/einen Beha/ein Kleid/einen Pullover
I need a coat/raincoat/jacket	Ich brauche einen Mantel/Regenmantel/eine Jacke
Do you sell buttons/elastic/zips?	Verkaufen Sie Knöpfe/Gummiband/Reissverschlüsse?
I need a pair of walking shoes/beach sandals/black shoes	Ich brauche ein Paar Strassenschuhe/Strandsandalen/schwarze Schuhe
These heels are too high/too low	Diese Absätze sind zu hoch/zu niedrig

Clothing sizes

WOMEN'S DRESSES, ETC.

British	32	34	36	38	40	42	44
American	10	12	14	16	18	20	22
Continental	30	32	34	36	38	40	42

MEN'S PULLOVERS, ETC.

British and American	36	38	40	42	44	46
Continental	46	48	50	52	54	56

MEN'S SHIRTS:

British and American	13	13½	14	14½	15	15½	15¾	16	16½	17	17½
Continental	34	35	36	37	38	39	40	41	42	43	44

MEN'S SOCKS:

British and American	10	10½	11	11½	12
Continental	39–40	41–42	43–44	45–46	47–48

STOCKINGS:

British and American	8	8½	9	9½	10	10½	11
Continental	0	1	2	3	4	5	6

SHOES:

British	1	2	3	4	5	6	7	8	9	10	11	12
American	2½	3½	4½	5½	6½	7½	8½	9½	10½	11½	12½	13½
Continental	33	34/5	36	37	38	39/40	41	42	43	44	45	46

Food[1]

Give me a kilo/half a kilo (pound) of . . . please	Geben Sie mir bitte ein Kilo/ ein halbes Kilo (ein Pfund) . . .
I want some sweets/chocolates, please	Ich möchte bitte Bonbons/ Pralinen
A bottle of milk/wine/beer, please	Eine Flasche Milch/Wein/Bier bitte
Is there anything back on the bottle?	Bekomme ich für die Flasche Pfand zurück?
I want a jar/tin (can)/packet of . . .	Ich möchte ein Glas/eine Dose/ ein Paket . . .
Do you sell frozen foods?	Verkaufen Sie Tiefkühlkost?
These pears are too hard/soft	Diese Birnen sind zu hart/weich
Is it fresh?	Ist es frisch?
Are they ripe?	Sind sie reif?
This is bad/stale	Dies ist schlecht/alt
A loaf of bread, please	Ein Brot bitte
Dark ryebread	Vollkornbrot/Schwarzbrot
Ryebread	Graubrot
White bread	Weissbrot
How much a kilo/bottle?	Wie teuer ist ein Kilo/eine Flasche?

1. See also the various MENU sections (p. 94 onward) and WEIGHTS AND MEASURES, pp. 173–4.

Hairdresser and barber

May I make an appointment for this morning/tomorrow afternoon?	Kann ich mich für heute morgen/morgen nachmittag anmelden?
What time?	Zu welcher Zeit?
I want my hair cut	Ich möchte mir die Haare schneiden lassen
I want my hair trimmed	Schneiden Sie mein Haar bitte nur ein wenig kürzer
Not too short at the sides	Nicht zu kurz an den Seiten
I'll have it shorter at the back, please	Hinten möchte ich es bitte kürzer haben
My hair is oily/dry	Mein Haar ist fettig/trocken
I want a shampoo	Waschen bitte
I want my hair washed and set	Waschen und legen bitte
Please set it without rollers/on large/small rollers	Bitte legen Sie es ohne Lockenwickler/auf grosse/kleine Lockenwickler
Please do not use any hairspray	Bitte benutzen Sie keinen Haarspray
I want a colour rinse	Ich möchte einen Farbfestiger
I'd like to see a colour chart	Kann ich bitte eine Farbskala sehen
I want a darker/lighter shade	Ich möchte einen dunkleren/helleren Farbton

I'd like it set this way, please — Ich möchte es bitte so gelegt haben

The water is too cold — Das Wasser ist zu kalt

The dryer is too hot — Die Trockenhaube ist zu heiss

Thank you, I like it very much — Danke, so gefällt es mir gut

I want a shave/manicure — Ich möchte mich rasieren/maniküren lassen

Hardware

Where is the camping equipment? — Wo ist die Camping/Zelt Ausrüstung?

Do you have a battery for this? — Haben Sie hierfür eine Batterie?

Where can I get butane gas/paraffin? — Wo kann ich Butan Gas/Petroleum bekommen?

I need a bottle opener/tin opener/corkscrew — Ich brauche einen Flaschenöffner/Dosenöffner/Korkenzieher

A small/large screwdriver — Ein kleiner/grosser Schraubenzieher

I'd like some candles/matches — Ich möchte Kerzen/Streichhölzer

I want a flashlight/(pen) knife/pair of scissors — Ich möchte eine Taschenlampe/ein (Taschen)messer/eine Schere

Do you sell string/rope?	Verkaufen Sie Band/Tau?
Where can I find washing-up liquid/scouring powder/soap pads?	Wo finde ich Abwaschseife/ Scheuersand/Seifenkissen?
Do you have a dishcloth/brush?	Haben Sie ein Geschirrtuch/ eine Bürste?
I need a groundsheet/bucket/ frying pan	Ich brauche eine Zeltbahn/ einen Eimer/eine Bratpfanne

Laundry and dry cleaning

Where is the nearest launderette/ dry cleaner?	Wo ist die nächste Schnellwäscherei/Reinigung?
I want to have these things washed/cleaned	Ich möchte diese Sachen waschen lassen/reinigen lassen
These stains won't come out	*Diese Flecken gehen nicht raus
Can you get this stain out?	Können Sie diesen Flecken rausmachen?
It is coffee/wine/grease	Es ist Kaffee/Wein/Fett
When will they be ready?	Wann sind sie fertig?
It only needs to be pressed	Es muss nur geplättet (gebügelt) werden
This is torn, can you mend it?	Dies ist zerrissen, können Sie es ausbessern?
Do you do invisible mending?	Machen Sie Kunststopfen?

There's a button missing	Hier fehlt ein Knopf
Will you sew on another one, please?	Würden Sie bitte einen anderen annähen?
I need them by this evening/ tomorrow	Ich brauche sie bis heute Abend/ Morgen
Call back at five o'clock	*Kommen Sie um fünf Uhr wieder
We can't do it until Tuesday	*Wir können es nicht vor Dienstag machen
It will take three days	*Es dauert drei Tage

Newspapers, writing materials and records

Do you sell English/American newspapers/magazines?	Verkaufen Sie englische/ amerikanische Zeitungen/ Zeitschriften?
Can you get . . . magazine for me?	Können Sie die Zeitschrift . . . für mich besorgen?
Where can I get the . . .?	Wo kann ich . . . bekommen?
I want a map of the city/road map of . . .	Ich möchte einen Stadtplan/ Strassenplan von . . .
I want an entertainment/ amusements guide	Ich möchte ein Veranstaltungsprogramm
Do you have any English books?	Haben Sie englische Bücher?

Have you any books by . . .?	Haben Sie irgendwelche Bücher von . . .?
I want some picture postcards/ plain postcards	Ich möchte einige Ansichtskarten/Postkarten
Do you sell souvenirs/toys?	Verkaufen Sie Reiseandenken/ Spielwaren?
Do you have any records of local music?	Haben Sie Platten mit hiesiger Musik?
Can I listen to this record, please?	Kann ich mir bitte diese Platte anhören?
Are there any new records by . . .	Gibt es neue Platten von . . .?
ballpoint	der Kugelschreiber
cellotape	Tesafilm
drawing pin	die Reisszwecke
elastic band	das Gummiband
envelope	der Umschlag, das Kuvert
glue/paste	der Leim/Klebstoff
ink	die Tinte
(coloured) pencil	der Bleistift (Farbstift)
string	das Band
(writing) paper	das (Schreib)papier

Photography

I want to buy a camera	Ich möchte eine Kamera kaufen
Have you a film/cartridge for this camera, please?	Haben Sie einen Film/eine Filmpatrone für diesen (Foto)apparat?
A 120/126 spool film, please, with 20/36 exposures	Einen hundert zwanzig/hundert sechsundzwanzig Film, bitte, mit zwanzig/sechsunddreissig Aufnahmen
Give me an 8/16/35 mm film, please	Geben Sie mir bitte einen acht/ sechzehn/fünfunddreissig Millimeter Film
I want a (fast) colour film/ black-and-white film	Ich möchte einen (schnellen) Farbfilm/schwarz-weiss Film
Would you fit the film in the camera for me, please	Würden Sie bitte den Film für mich in den Apparat einlegen
Do you have flash bulbs/cubes?	Haben Sie Blitzlampen/ Blitzwürfel?
Does the price include processing?	Schliesst dieser Preis das Entwickeln ein?
I'd like this film developed and printed	Würden Sie diesen Film bitte entwickeln und abziehen?
Please enlarge this negative	Bitte machen Sie eine Vergrösserung von diesem Negativ
When will it be ready?	Wann ist es fertig?

Will it be done tomorrow?	Ist es morgen fertig?
My camera's not working, can you mend it?	Meine Kamera funktioniert nicht, können Sie sie reparieren?
The film is jammed	Der Film hat sich festgeklemmt
There is something wrong with the shutter/light meter/film winder	Es stimmt etwas nicht mit dem Verschluss/Belichtungsmesser/Transportknopf
I need a (haze) filter/lens cap	Ich brauche einen (Dunst) Filter/Objektivdeckel

Tobacconist

Do you stock English/American cigarettes?	Haben Sie englische/amerikanische Zigaretten?
What cigarettes/cigars have you?	Welche Zigaretten/Zigarren haben Sie?
A packet of . . . please	Eine Schachtel . . . bitte
I want some filter tip cigarettes/cigarettes without filter/menthol cigarettes	Ich möchte Filterzigaretten/Zigaretten ohne Filter/Zigaretten mit Menthol
A box of matches, please	Eine Schachtel Streichhölzer bitte
Do you have cigarette paper/pipe cleaners?	Haben Sie Zigarettenpapier/Pfeifenreiniger?

I want to buy a lighter	Ich möchte ein Feuerzeug kaufen
Do you sell lighter fuel/flints?	Verkaufen Sie Feuerzeug-Benzin/Flintsteine?
I want a gas refill	Ich möchte eine neue Gasfüllung

Repairs

This is broken; could you mend it?	Dies ist kaputt; können Sie es reparieren?
Could you do it while I wait?	Können Sie es machen, während ich warte?
When should I come back for it?	Wann kann ich es abholen?
I want these shoes soled (with leather)	Ich möchte an diesen Schuhen (Leder)sohlen haben
I want them heeled (with rubber)	Ich möchte an ihnen (Gummi)absätze haben
I have broken the heel; can you put on a new one?	Der Absatz ist gebrochen; können Sie einen neuen anmachen?
My watch is broken	Meine Uhr ist kaputt
I have broken the glass/strap/spring	Das Glas/der Riemen/die Feder ist kaputt
I have broken my glasses/the frame/the arm	Meine Brille/der Rahmen/der Bügel ist kaputt

How much would a new one cost?	Wieviel kostet ein neuer/eine neue/ein neues?
The stone/charm/screw has come loose	Der Stein/der Anhänger/die Schraube ist lose
The fastener/clip/chain is broken	Der Verschluss/die Spange/die Kette ist kaputt
It can't be repaired	*Es kann nicht repariert werden

Post Office

Where's the main post office?	Wo ist die Hauptpost?
Where's the nearest post office?	Wo ist die nächste Post?
What time does the post office open/close?	Wann macht die Post auf/zu?
Where's the post box?	Wo ist der Briefkasten?
Which window do I go to for stamps/money orders?	An welchem Fenster bekomme ich Briefmarken/ Postanweisungen?
Where can I send a telegram?	Wo kann ich ein Telegram aufgeben?

Letters and telegrams

How much is a postcard to England?	Wie teuer ist eine Postkarte nach England?
What's the airmail to the USA?	Wie teuer ist Luftpost in die USA?
How much is it to send a letter surface mail to the USA?	Wie teuer ist ein Brief per Schiffpost in die USA?
It's inland	Es ist fürs Inland
Give me three . . . pfennig stamps, please	Geben Sie mir bitte drei Briefmarken zu . . . Pfennig
I want to send this letter express	Ich möchte diesen Brief per Eilpost senden
I want to register this letter	Ich möchte diesen Brief einschreiben
Two airmail forms, please	Zwei Luftpostbriefe bitte
Where is the poste restante section?	Wo ist der Schalter 'Postlagernde Sendungen'?
Are there any letters for me?	Sind Briefe für mich da?
What is your name?	*Wie ist Ihr Name?
Have you any means of identification?	*Können Sie sich identifizieren (ausweisen)?
I want to send a (reply paid) telegram/night letter	Ich möchte ein Telegramm (mit bezahlter Antwort)/ein Brieftelegramm senden

How much does it cost per word?	Wieviel kostet es pro Wort?
Write the message here and your own name and address	*Schreiben Sie den Text hier und Ihren eigenen Namen und Adresse

Telephoning

Where's the nearest phone box?	Wo ist die nächste Telefonzelle?
I want to make a phone call	Ich möchte telefonieren
May I use your phone?	Kann ich Ihr Telefon benutzen?
Do you have a telephone directory for . . .?	Haben Sie ein Telefonbuch für . . .?
Please get me . . .	Bitte verbinden Sie mich mit . . .
I want to telephone to England	Ich möchte nach England telefonieren
I want to make a personal (person-to-person) call	Ich möchte ein V-Gespräch führen (*pronounce* V *as vow*)
Could you give me the cost (time and charges) afterwards?	Könnten Sie mir hinterher die Gebühren angeben?
I want to reverse the charges (call collect)	Ein R-Gespräch bitte (*pronounce* R *as air*)
I was cut off; can you reconnect me?	Ich wurde unterbrochen; können Sie mich wieder verbinden?
I want extension . . .	Apparat . . . bitte

May I speak to . . .	Kann ich bitte . . . sprechen
Who's speaking?	*Wer spricht da?
Hold the line, please	*Bleiben Sie bitte am Apparat
Put the receiver down	*Legen Sie den Hörer auf
He's not here	*Er ist nicht hier
When will he be back?	Wann kommt er zurück?
Will you take a message?	Würden Sie bitte etwas ausrichten?
Tell him that . . . phoned	Sagen Sie ihm bitte, dass . . . angerufen hat
I'll ring again later	Ich rufe später wieder an
Please ask him to phone me	Bitten Sie ihn, mich anzurufen
What's your number?	*Wie ist Ihre Nummer?
My number is . . .	Meine Nummer ist . . .
I can't hear you	Ich kann Sie nicht verstehen
The line is engaged	*Die Leitung ist besetzt
There's no reply	*Es meldet sich niemand
You have the wrong number	*Sie sind falsch verbunden

Sightseeing[1]

What ought one to see here?	Was ist hier sehenswert?
Is there a sightseeing tour/boat ride?	Gibt es eine Stadtrundfahrt/ Bootsfahrt?
What's this building?	Was ist das für ein Gebäude?
Which is the oldest building in the city?	Welches ist das älteste Gebäude in der Stadt?
When was it built?	Wann wurde es gebaut?
Who built it?	Wer hat es gebaut?
What's the name of this church?	Wie heisst diese Kirche?
Is this the natural history museum?	Ist dies das Naturkunde- Museum?
When is the museum open?	Wann ist das Museum geöffnet?
Is it open on Sundays?	Ist es sonntags geöffnet?
The museum is closed on Mondays	*Das Museum ist montags geschlossen

1. See also BUS and COACH TRAVEL (p. 54), DIRECTIONS (p. 57).

Admission free	*Eintritt frei
How much is it to go in?	Wieviel Eintritt kostet es?
Are there reductions for children/ students?	Gibt es Ermässigung für Kinder/Studenten?
Are the entry fees reduced on any special day?	Gibt es an bestimmten Tagen eine Eintrittsermässigung?
Have you a ticket?	*Haben Sie eine Eintrittskarte?
Where do I get tickets?	Wo bekomme ich Eintrittskarten?
Please leave your bag in the cloakroom	*Bitte lassen Sie Ihre Tasche in der Garderobe
It's over there	*Es ist dort drüben
Can I take pictures?	Kann ich fotografieren?
Photographs are prohibited	*Fotografieren ist verboten
Follow the guide	*Folgen Sie dem Führer
Does the guide speak English?	Spricht der Führer englisch?
We don't need a guide	Wir brauchen keinen Führer
Where is the ... collection/ exhibition?	Wo ist die Sammlung/ Ausstellung ...?
Where are the Rembrandts?	Wo sind die Rembrandts?
Where can I get a catalogue?	Wo kann ich einen Katalog bekommen?
Where can I get a plan/guide book of the city?	Wo kann ich einen Stadtplan/ Stadtführer bekommen?
Is this the way to the zoo?	Komme ich hier zum Zoo?
Which bus goes to the castle?	Welcher Bus fährt zum Schloss?

How do I get to the park?	Wie komme ich zum Park?
Where do we find antiques/souvenirs/a shopping centre/the market?	Wo gibt es Antiquitäten/Reiseandenken/ein Einkaufszentrum/den Markt?
Can we walk it?	Können wir zu Fuss gehen?

Entertainment

Is there an entertainment guide?	Gibt es ein Veranstaltungs-programm?
What's on at the theatre/cinema?	Was wird im Theater/im Kino gespielt?
Is there a concert on?	Gibt es ein Konzert?
I want two seats for tonight/for the matinee tomorrow	Ich möchte zwei Plätze für heute Abend/für die Matinee-Vorstellung morgen
I want to book seats for Thursday	Ich möchte Plätze für Donnerstag bestellen
That performance is sold out	*Die Vorstellung ist ausverkauft
Are they good seats?	Sind es gute Plätze?
Where are these seats?	Wo sind diese Plätze?
When does the curtain go up?	Wann geht der Vorhang auf?
What time does the performance end?	Wann ist die Vorstellung zu Ende?
Is evening dress necessary?	Ist Abendkleidung erforderlich?

Where is the cloakroom?	Wo ist die Garderobe?
This is your seat	*Hier ist Ihr Platz
A programme, please	Ein Programm bitte
What's the best nightclub?	Welches ist der beste Nachtklub?
What time is the floorshow?	Wann beginnt das Kabarett?
May I have this dance?	Darf ich Sie um diesen Tanz bitten?
Is there a jazz club here?	Gibt es hier einen Jazz Club?
Do you have a discotheque here?	Haben Sie hier eine Diskothek?
Can you recommend a good show?	Können Sie eine gute Veranstaltung empfehlen?

Sports and games

Where is the nearest tennis court/golf course?	Wo ist der nächste Tennisplatz/Golfplatz?
What is the charge per game/hour/day?	Wieviel kostet es pro Spiel/Stunde/Tag?
Where can we go swimming/fishing?	Wo können wir schwimmen/angeln?
Can I hire a racket/clubs/fishing tackle?	Kann ich einen Tennisschläger/Golfschläger/ein Angelgerät mieten?
I want to go fishing; do I need a permit?	Ich möchte angeln gehen; brauche ich einen Angelschein?
Where do I get a permit?	Wo bekomme ich einen (Angel)schein?
Is there a skating rink/ski slope?	Gibt es eine Eisbahn/einen Skiabhang?
Can I hire skates/skiing equipment?	Kann ich Schlittschuhe/eine Skiausrüstung leihen?

Are there ski lifts?	Gibt es Skilifts?
Can I take lessons here?	Kann ich hier Unterricht nehmen?
Where is the stadium?	Wo ist das Stadion?
Are there any seats left in the grandstand?	Gibt es noch Plätze auf der Haupttribüne?
How much are the cheapest seats?	Wieviel kosten die billigsten Plätze?
Are the seats in the sun/shade?	Sind die Plätze in der Sonne/im Schatten?
We want to go to a football match/a tennis tournament	Wir möchten uns ein Fussballspiel/ein Tennisturnier ansehen
Who's playing?	Wer spielt?
When does it start?	Wann fängt es an?
What is the score?	Wie steht's?
Who's winning?	Wer gewinnt?
Where's the race course?	Wo ist die Rennbahn?
When's the next meeting?	Wann ist das nächste Rennen?
Which is the favourite?	Wer ist der Favorit?
Who's the jockey?	Wer ist der Jockey?
20 DM to win on . . ./each way on . . .	Zwanzig Mark Siegwette auf . . ./ Sieg- und Platzwette auf . . .
What are the odds?	Wie ist der Wettkurs?
Do you play cards?	Spielen Sie Karten?
Would you like a game of chess?	Möchten Sie Schach spielen?

On the beach

Which is the best beach?	Welches ist der beste Strand?
Is there a quiet beach near here?	Gibt es einen ruhigen Strand in der Nähe?
Is it far to walk?	Ist es weit zu gehen?
Is there a bus to the beach?	Fährt ein Bus zum Strand?
Is the beach sand/pebbles/rocks?	Ist es ein Sand-/Kies-/Felsstrand?
Is the bathing safe from this beach/bay?	Ist das Baden an diesem Strand/in dieser Bucht ungefährlich?
Is it safe for small children?	Können kleine Kinder hier ohne Gefahr baden?
Bathing prohibited/at own risk	*Baden verboten/auf eigene Gefahr
Does it get very rough?	Wird das Wasser sehr bewegt?
It's dangerous	*Es ist gefährlich
Is the tide rising/falling?	Steigt/fällt das Wasser?

There's a strong current here	*Die Strömung ist hier sehr stark
It's very deep here	*Es ist hier sehr tief
Are you a strong swimmer?	*Sind Sie ein tüchtiger Schwimmer?
Is it deep?	Ist es tief?
How's the water? Cold?	Wie ist das Wasser? Kalt?
It's warm	Es ist warm
Can one swim in the lake/river?	Kann man im See/im Fluss baden?
Is there an indoor/outdoor swimming pool?	Gibt es ein Hallenbad/ein Freibad?
Is it salt or fresh water?	Ist es Salz- oder Süsswasser?
Are there showers?	Gibt es Duschen?
I want to hire a cabin for the day/morning/two hours	Ich mochte eine Kabine mieten für den Tag/für den Morgen/für zwei Stunden
I want to hire a deckchair/a sunshade	Ich möchte einen Liegestuhl/Sonnenschirm mieten
Can we water ski here?	Können wir hier Wasserski laufen?
Can we hire the equipment?	Können wir die Ausrüstung mieten?
Where's the harbour?	Wo ist der Hafen?
Can we go out in a fishing boat?	Können wir in einem Fischkutter hinausfahren?

Is there any underwater fishing?	Kann man unter Wasser fischen?
Can I hire skin-diving equipment/a snorkel/flippers?	Kann ich eine Tauchausrüstung/einen Schnorchel/Schwimmflossen mieten?
Can I hire a rowing/motor/sailing boat?	Kann ich ein Ruderboot/Motorboot/Segelboot mieten?
What does it cost by the hour?	Wieviel kostet ein Boot pro Stunde?

Camping and walking[1]

How long is the walk to the Youth Hostel?	Wie lange geht man zur Jugendherberge?
How far is the next village?	Wie weit ist es bis zum nächsten Dorf?
Is there a footpath to . . .?	Gibt es einen Wanderweg nach . . .?
Is it possible to go across country?	Kann man feldein gehen?
Is there a short cut?	Gibt es einen kürzeren Weg?
It's an hour's walk to . . .	*Man geht eine Stunde nach . . .
Is there a camping site near here?	Gibt es einen Zeltplatz in der Nähe?
Is this an authorized camp site?	Ist das Zelten hier erlaubt?
Are drinking water/lavatories/showers provided?	Gibt es Trinkwasser/Toiletten/Duschen?
May we camp here?	Dürfen wir hier zelten?

1. See also DIRECTIONS (p. 57).

Can we hire a tent?	Können wir ein Zelt mieten?
Can we park our caravan here?	Können wir unseren Wohnwagen hier parken?
What does it cost per person/day/week?	Was kostet es pro Person/Tag/Woche?
What is the charge for a tent/caravan?	Wie hoch ist die Gebühr für ein Zelt/einen Wohnwagen?
Is this drinking water?	Ist dies Trinkwasser?
Where are the shops?	Wo sind die Geschäfte?
Where can I buy paraffin/butane gas?	Wo kann ich Petroleum/Butan (Gas) kaufen?
May we light a fire?	Dürfen wir ein Feuer anzünden?
Where do I get rid of rubbish?	Wo kann ich den Abfall hintun?

At the doctor's

Ailments

Is there a doctor's surgery near here?	Gibt es hier in der Nähe eine Arztpraxis?
I must see a doctor, can you recommend one?	Ich muss zum Arzt, können Sie mir einen empfehlen?
Please call a doctor	Bitte, rufen Sie einen Arzt
I am ill	Ich bin krank
I have a fever	Ich habe Fieber
I've a pain in my right arm	Ich habe Schmerzen im rechten Arm
My wrist hurts	Mein Handgelenk tut mir weh
I think I've sprained my ankle/ broken my ankle	Ich glaube, ich habe mir den Fuss verstaucht/den Knöchel gebrochen
I fell down and hurt my back	Ich bin hingefallen und habe mir den Rücken verletzt

My foot is swollen	Mein Fuss ist geschwollen
I've burned/cut/bruised myself	Ich habe mich verbrannt/geschnitten/gestossen, gequetscht
My stomach is upset	Ich habe Magenbeschwerden
My appetite's gone	Ich habe den Appetit verloren
I think I've got food poisoning	Ich glaube, ich habe eine Lebensmittelvergiftung
I can't eat/sleep	Ich kann nicht essen/nicht schlafen
My nose keeps bleeding	Meine Nase blutet immer
I have difficulty in breathing	Ich habe Schwierigkeiten beim Atmen
I feel dizzy/sick	Mir ist schwindlig/schlecht
I feel shivery	Mich fröstelt
I keep vomiting	Ich muss mich immer übergeben
I think I've caught 'flu	Ich glaube, ich habe Grippe
I've got a cold	Ich habe eine Erkältung
I've had it since yesterday/for a few hours	Ich habe es seit gestern/ein paar Stunden

abscess	das Geschwür	**geshvuir**
ache	der Schmerz	shmairts
allergy	die Allergie	ullairgee
appendicitis	die Blinddarm-Entzündung	**blint**dahrm-enttsuindōong

asthma	das Asthma	**ust**mah
blister	die Blase	**blah**zer
boil	der Furunkel	foo**roon**kel
bruise	die Quetschung	**kvet**shoong
burn	die Brandwunde	**brunt**voonder
cardiac condition	der Herzfehler	**hairts**-faylair
chill, cold	die Erkältung	air**kail**toong
constipation	die Verstopfung	fair**shtopf**oong
cough	der Husten	**hoo**sten
cramp	der Krampf	**crumpf**
diabetic	zuckerkrank	**tsook**ercrunk
diarrhoea	der Durchfall	**doorkh**ful
earache	die Ohrenschmerzen	**ohren**shmairtsen
fever	das Fieber	**fee**bair
food poisoning	die Lebensmittel-Vergiftung	**lay**bensmittel-fair**gift**oong
fracture	der Bruch	**brookh**
hay-fever	der Heuschnupfen	**hoy**shnoopfen
headache	die Kopfschmerzen	**copf**shmairtsen
ill, sick	krank	**crunk**
illness	die Krankheit	**crunk**hite
indigestion	die Verdauungs-Störung	fair**dow**oongs-shter-roong
infection	die Ansteckung	**un**shteckoong

influenza	die Grippe	gripper
insomnia	die Schlaflosigkeit	**shlahf**-lohsikh-kite
itch	das Jucken	yŏoken
nausea	die Übelkeit	**ui**bel-kite
pain	der Schmerz	shmairts
rheumatism	der Rheumatismus	rŏomatizmŏos
sore throat	die Halsschmerzen	**huls**-shmairtsen
sprain	die Verstauchung	fair**shtow**khŏong
stomach ache	die Magenschmerzen	**mah**gen-shmairtsen
sunburn	der Sonnenbrand	**zon**nen-brunt
sunstroke	der Sonnenstich	**zon**nen-shtikh
tonsillitis	die Mandel-entzündung	**mund**el-enttsuindŏong
toothache	die Zahnschmerzen	**tsahn**-shmairtsen
ulcer	das Geschwür	gesh**vuir**
wound	die Wunde	vŏonder

Treatment

You're hurting me	Sie tun mir weh
Must I stay in bed?	Muss ich im Bett bleiben?
Will you call again?	Kommen Sie wieder?
How much do I owe you?	Wieviel schulde ich Ihnen?

When can I travel again?	Wann kann ich wieder reisen?
I feel better now	Mir geht es jetzt wieder besser
Do you have a temperature?	*Haben Sie erhöhte Temperatur?
Where does it hurt?	*Wo tut es weh?
Have you a pain here?	*Haben Sie hier Schmerzen?
How long have you had the pain?	*Seit wann haben Sie die Schmerzen?
Does that hurt?	*Tut das weh?
A lot?	*Sehr?
A little?	*Ein wenig?
Open your mouth	*Machen Sie den Mund auf
Put out your tongue	*Stecken Sie die Zunge raus
Breathe in/out	*Atmen Sie ein/aus
Please lie down	*Legen Sie sich bitte hin
I will need a specimen	*Ich brauche eine Urinprobe
What medicines have you been taking?	*Welche Medikamente haben Sie eingenommen?
I take this medicine; could you give me another prescription?	Ich nehme dieses Medikament ein; können Sie mir noch ein Rezept geben?
I'll give you some pills/tablets/medicine	*Ich werde Ihnen Pillen/Tabletten/Arznei (Medizin) geben
I will give you an antibiotic/sedative	*Ich gebe Ihnen ein Antibiotikum/ein Beruhigungsmittel

Take this prescription to the chemist's	*Bringen Sie dieses Rezept in die Apotheke
Take this three times a day	*Nehmen Sie dies dreimal täglich ein
I'll give you an injection	*Ich gebe Ihnen eine Spritze
Roll up your sleeve	*Rollen Sie den Ärmel auf
I'll put you on a diet	*Ich werde Sie auf Diät setzen
Come and see me again in two days' time	*Kommen Sie in zwei Tagen wieder
Your leg must be X-rayed	*Ihr Bein muss geröntgt werden
You must go to hospital	*Sie müssen ins Krankenhaus
You must stay in bed	*Sie müssen im Bett bleiben
You should not travel until ...	*Sie sollten bis ... nicht reisen
Nothing to worry about	*Es besteht kein Grund zur Unruhe

ambulance	der Krankenwagen	**crun**ken-**vah**gen
anaesthetic	das Betäubungsmittel	betoyb**oo**ngs-mittell
aspirin	das Aspirin	uspee**reen**
bandage	der Verband	fair**bunt**
chiropodist	der Fusspfleger	f**oo**s-pflaygair
hospital	das Krankenhaus	**crun**kenhows
injection	die Spritze	shprittser
laxative	das Abführmittel	**up**fuir-mittell
nurse	die (Kranken)-schwester	(**crun**ken)shvester

operation	die Operation	operats-**yohn**
optician	der Optiker	**op**teekair
osteopath	der Knochen- heilkundige	**k-no**khen- hilek**oo**ndiger
pill	die Tablette	**tub**letter
(adhesive) plaster	das Pflaster	**pflus**tair
prescription	das Rezept	ret**sept**
X-ray	die Röntgenaufnahme	**rernt**gen-owfnahmer

Parts of the body

ankle	der Fussknöchel	**foos**-knerkhell
arm	der Arm	ahrm
back	der Rücken	**rui**ken
bladder	die Blase	**blah**ser
blood	das Blut	bl**oo**t
body	der Körper	**ker**pair
bone	der Knochen	**k-no**khen
bowels	der Darm	darm
brain	das Gehirn	ge**heern**
breast	die Brust	br**oo**st
cheek	die Wange	**vun**ger
chest	die Brust	br**oo**st

chin	das Kinn	kin
collar-bone	das Schlüsselbein	**shlui**sselbine
ear	das Ohr	ohr
elbow	der Ellbogen	**el**bohgen
eye	das Auge	**ow**ger
eyelid	das Augenlid	**ow**genlid
face	das Gesicht	ge**zikht**
finger	der Finger	**finger**
foot	der Fuss	fo͠os
forehead	die Stirn	shteern
gums	das Zahnfleisch	**zahn**fleisch
hand	die Hand	hunt
head	der Kopf	copf
heart	das Herz	hairts
heel	die Ferse	fairzer
hip	die Hüfte	huifter
jaw	der Kiefer	keefer
joint	das Gelenk	ge**lenk**
kidney	die Niere	neerer
knee	das Knie	k-nee
knee-cap	die Kniescheibe	**k-nee**shiber
leg	das Bein	bine
lip	die Lippe	lipper
liver	die Leber	**lay**bair

lung	die Lunge	lŏŏnger
mouth	der Mund	mŏŏnt
muscle	der Muskel	**mŏŏ**skell
nail	der Nagel	**nah**gell
neck	der Hals	huls
nerve	der Nerv	nairf
nose	die Nase	nahzer
rib	die Rippe	ripper
shoulder	die Schulter	**schŏŏl**tair
skin	die Haut	howt
stomach	der Magen	mahgen
temple	die Schläfe	shlefer
thigh	der Schenkel	**shen**kel
throat	der Hals	huls
thumb	der Daumen	dowmen
toe	der Zeh	tsay
tongue	die Zunge	tsŏŏnger
tonsils	die Mandeln	**mun**deln
tooth	der Zahn	tsahn
vein	die Ader	**ah**dair
wrist	das Handgelenk	**hunt**-gelenk

At the dentist's

I must see a dentist	Ich muss zum Zahnarzt
Can I make an appointment?	Kann ich mich anmelden?
As soon as possible, please	Sobald wie möglich bitte
I have toothache	Ich habe Zahnschmerzen
This tooth hurts	Dieser Zahn tut weh
I've lost a filling	Ich habe eine Füllung (Plombe) verloren
Can you fill it?	Können Sie ihn plombieren (füllen)?
Can you do it now?	Können Sie es jetzt machen?
I do not want the tooth taken out	Ziehen Sie den Zahn bitte nicht raus
Please give me an injection first	Bitte geben Sie mir zuerst eine Spritze (örtliche Betäubung)
My gums are swollen/keep bleeding	Mein Zahnfleisch ist geschwollen/blutet immer

I have broken/chipped my dentures	Meine Zahnprotese ist zerbrochen/angeschlagen
Can you fix it (temporarily)?	Können Sie sie (vorläufig) reparieren?
You're hurting me	Sie tun mir weh
How much do I owe you?	Wieviel schulde ich Ihnen?
When should I come again?	Wann soll ich wiederkommen?
Please rinse your mouth	*Bitte spülen Sie den Mund aus
I will X-ray your teeth	*Ich werde Ihre Zähne röntgen
You have an abscess	*Sie haben ein Geschwür (einen Abzess)
The nerve is exposed	*Der Nerv ist blossgelegt
This tooth can't be saved	*Dieser Zahn ist nicht zu retten

Problems and accidents

Where's the police station?	Wo ist die Polizeiwache?
Call the police	Rufen Sie die Polizei
Where is the British consulate?	Wo ist das britische Konsulat?
Please let the consulate know	Bitte benachrichtigen Sie das Konsulat
My bag has been stolen	Man hat mir meine Tasche gestohlen
I found this in the street	Ich habe dies auf der Strasse gefunden
I have lost my luggage/passport/ travellers' cheques	Ich habe mein Gepäck/meinen Pass/meine Reiseschecks verloren
I have missed my train	Ich habe meinen Zug verpasst
My luggage is on board	Mein Gepäck ist an Bord
Call a doctor	Rufen Sie einen Arzt
Call an ambulance	Rufen Sie einen Krankenwagen
There has been an accident	Ein Unfall hat sich ereignet

He's badly hurt	Er ist schwer verletzt
He has fainted	Er ist ohnmächtig geworden
He's losing blood	Er verliert Blut
Please get some water/a blanket/some bandages	Bitte holen Sie etwas Wasser/eine Decke/Verbandszeug
I've broken my glasses	Meine Brille ist kaputt
I can't see	Ich kann nichts sehen
A child has fallen in the water	Ein Kind ist ins Wasser gefallen
A woman is drowning	Eine Frau ist am Ertrinken
May I see your insurance certificate?	*Ich möchte Ihren Versicherungsschein sehen
Apply to the insurance company	*Wenden Sie sich an die Versicherungsgesellschaft
Can you help me?	Können Sie mir helfen?
What are the name and address of the owner?	Wie ist der Name und die Adresse des Besitzers?
Are you willing to act as a witness?	Sind Sie bereit, als Zeuge aufzutreten?
Can I have your name and address, please?	Ihren Namen und Ihre Adresse, bitte
I want a copy of the police report	Ich möchte eine Kopie des Polizeiberichts
There's a bus strike/go slow	*Die Busfahrer sind in den Streik/einen Bummelstreik getreten

Time and dates

TIME

What time is it?	Wie spät ist es?
It's one o'clock	Es ist ein Uhr
two o'clock	zwei Uhr
five past eight[1]	fünf (Minuten) nach acht
quarter past five	Viertel nach fünf
twenty-five past eight	fünf vor halb neun
half past nine	halb zehn
twenty-five to seven	fünf nach halb sieben
twenty to three	zwanzig vor drei
quarter to ten	dreiviertel zehn
Second	die Sekunde
Minute	die Minute
Hour	die Stunde

1. The basic sequence is: five, ten, quarter *past*; ten, five *to half*; half *to next hour*; five, ten *past half*; quarter, ten, five *to next hour*.

It's early/late	Es ist früh/spät
My watch is slow/fast	Meine Uhr geht nach/vor
The clock has stopped	Die Uhr ist stehengeblieben
Sorry I'm late	Entschuldigen Sie die Verspätung

DATE

DATUM

What's the date?	Welches Datum ist heute?
It's December 9th	Es ist der neunte Dezember
We're leaving on January 5th	Wir fahren am fünften Januar ab
We got here on July 27th	Wir sind am siebenundzwanzigsten Juli angekommen

DAY · TAG

DAY	TAG	
Morning	der Morgen	**morgen**
this morning	heute Morgen	hoyter **morgen**
in the morning	am Morgen/ morgens	am **morgen**/ **morgen**s
Midday, noon	der Mittag	**mittahg**
at noon	zu Mittag	tsoo **mittahg**
Afternoon	der Nachmittag	**nahkh**mittahg
tomorrow afternoon	morgen nachmittag	morgen **nahkh**mittahg
Evening	der Abend	**ahbent**

Midnight	Mitternacht	**mitter**-nukht
Night	die Nacht	nukht
tonight	heute Abend	hoyter **ah**bent
last night	gestern Abend	gestairn **ah**bent
Sunrise	der Sonnenaufgang	zonnen-**owf**gung
Dawn	das Morgengrauen,	**mor**gen-growen/
	der Tagesanbruch	**tah**hes-an**brōōkh**
Sunset	der Sonnen-	zonnen-**ōōn**tairgung
	untergang	
Dusk, twilight	das Zwielicht	**tsweel**ikht
Today	heute	**hoy**ter
Yesterday	gestern	**gest**airn
two days ago	vorgestern	**for**gestairn
Tomorrow	morgen	**mor**gen
in two days	übermorgen	**ui**bermorgen
in three days	in drei Tagen	in dri **tah**gen

WEEK	WOCHE	**voh**ker
Monday	Montag	**mohn**tahg
Tuesday	Dienstag	**deens**tahg
Wednesday	Mittwoch	**mit**vokh
Thursday	Donnerstag	**donn**airstahg
Friday	Freitag	**fri**tahg

Saturday	Samstag/Sonnabend	**zum**stahg/**zon**ahbent
Sunday	Sonntag	**zon**tahg
on Tuesday	(am) Dienstag	(am) **deen**stahg
on Sundays	sonntags	**zon**tahgs
Fortnight	zwei Wochen/	tsvī vokhen/**feer**tsayn
	vierzehn Tage	tahger

MONTH	MONAT	**moh**naht
January	Januar	**yun**ōōahr
February	Februar	**feb**rōōahr
March	März	mairts
April	April	up**ril**
May	Mai	mī
June	Juni	**yoo**nee
July	Juli	**yoo**lee
August	August	ow**gōōst**
September	September	Sep**tem**bair
October	Oktober	Oc**toh**bair
November	November	noh**vem**bair
December	Dezember	dayt**sem**bair
in March	im März	im mairts

SEASON	JAHRESZEIT	**yahres-tsit**
Spring	der Frühling, das Frühjahr	**fruiling, fruiyahr**
Summer	der Sommer	**zommair**
Autumn	der Herbst	**hairbst**
Winter	der Winter	**vintair**
in spring	im Frühjahr	im **fruiyahr**
during the summer	während des Sommers	**vairent** des **zommers**

YEAR	JAHR	**yahr**
This year	dieses Jahr	**deezes yahr**
Last year	voriges/vergangenes Jahr	**foriges/fairgungenes yahr**
Next year	nächstes Jahr	**naykhstes yahr**

Public holidays

1 January	der Neujahrstag	New Year's Day
6 January	das Dreikönigsfest	Epiphany (Austria only)
	der Karfreitag	Good Friday
	der Ostermontag	Easter Monday
1 May	der Tag der Arbeit	Mayday (not Switzerland)
	der Himmelfahrtstag	Ascension Day
	der Pfingstmontag	Whit Monday
	der Fronleichnam	Corpus Christi (Austria only)
17 June	Siebzehnter Juni	(Germany only)
15 August	Mariä Himmelfahrt	Ascension of the Virgin (Austria only)
1 November	Allerheiligen	All Saints (Austria only)
16 November	Buss- und Bettag	(Germany only)
8 December	die unbefleckte Empfängnis	Conception Day (Austria only)
25 December	der (erste) Weihnachtstag	Christmas Day
26 December	der zweite Weihnachtstag	Boxing Day

Numbers

CARDINAL

0	null	nöol
1	eins	ines
2	zwei	tsvi
3	drei	dri
4	vier	feer
5	fünf	fuinf
6	sechs	zekhs
7	sieben	zeeben
8	acht	akht
9	neun	noyn
10	zehn	tsayn
11	elf	elf
12	zwölf	tsverlf
13	dreizehn	**drī**tsayn
14	vierzehn	**feer**tsayn

15	fünfzehn	**fuinf**tsayn
16	sechzehn	**zekh**tsayn
17	siebzehn	**zeeb**tsayn
18	achtzehn	**akht**sayn
19	neunzehn	**noynt**sayn
20	zwanzig	**tsvunt**sikh
21	einundzwanzig	**īn**-ŏŏnt-tsvuntsikh
22	zweiundzwanzig	**tsvī**-ŏŏnt-tsvuntsikh
30	dreissig	**drī**ssikh
31	einunddreissig	**īn**-ŏŏnt-dryssikh
32	zweiunddreissig	**tsvy**-ŏŏnt-dryssikh
40	vierzig	**feer**tsikh
41	einundvierzig	**īne**-ŏŏnt-feertsikh
50	fünfzig	**fuinf**tsikh
51	einundfünfzig	**īne**-ŏŏnt-fuinftsikh
60	sechzig	**zekh**tsikh
61	einundsechzig	**īne**-ŏŏnt-zekhtsikh
70	siebzig	**zeeb**tsikh
71	einundsiebzig	**īne**-ŏŏnt-zeebtsikh
80	achtzig	**akht**sikh
81	einundachtzig	**īne**-ŏŏnt-akhtsikh
90	neunzig	**noynt**sikh
91	einundneunzig	**īne**-ŏŏnt-noyntsikh
100	hundert	**hŏŏn**dert

101	hunderteins	hŏŏndertīns
200	zweihundert	tsvīhŏŏndert
1,000	tausend	**tow**zent
2,000	zweitausend	**tsvī**towzent
1,000,000	eine Million	**ī**ner meel**yohn**

ORDINAL

1st	der erste	airster
2nd	zweite	tsvīter
3rd	dritte	dritter
4th	vierte	feerter
5th	fünfte	fuinfter
6th	sechste	zekhster
7th	siebte	zeebter
8th	achte	akhter
9th	neunte	noynter
10th	zehnte	tsaynter
11th	elfte	elfter
12th	zwölfte	tsverlfter
13th	dreizehnte	**drī**tsaynter
14th	vierzehnte	**feer**tsaynter
15th	fünfzehnte	**fuinf**tsaynter
16th	sechzehnte	**zekh**tsaynter
17th	siebzehnte	**zeeb**tsaynter

18th	achtzehnte	**akht**saynter
19th	neunzehnte	**noynt**saynter
20th	zwanzigste	**tsvunt**sigster
21st	einundzwanzigste	**ine**-ŏŏnt-tsvuntsikh-ster
30th	dreissigste	**drĭ**ssikhster
40th	vierzigste	**feert**sikhster
50th	fünfzigste	**fuinft**sikhster
60th	sechzigste	**zekht**sikhster
70th	siebzigste	**zeebt**sikhster
80th	achtzigste	**akht**sikhster
90th	neunzigste	**noynt**sikhster
100th	hundertste	**hŏŏn**dertster
1000th	tausendste	**tow**zentster
half	(ein) halb	halp
quarter	(ein) Viertel	**feer**tel
three quarters	dreiviertel	**drĭ**feertel
a third	ein Drittel	**drit**tel
two thirds	zwei Drittel	**tsvĭ** drittel

Weights and measures

DISTANCE

kilometres – miles

km	*miles or km*	miles	km	*miles or km*	miles
1·6	*1*	0·6	14·5	*9*	5·6
3·2	*2*	1·2	16·1	*10*	6·2
4·8	*3*	1·9	32·2	*20*	12·4
6·4	*4*	2·5	40·2	*25*	15·3
8	*5*	3·1	80·5	*50*	31·1
9·7	*6*	3·7	160·9	*100*	62·1
11·3	*7*	4·4	402·3	*250*	155·3
12·9	*8*	5·0	804·7	*500*	310·7

A rough way to convert from miles to kms: divide by 5 and multiply by 8; from kms to miles divide by 8 and multiply by 5.

LENGTH AND HEIGHT

centimetres – inches

cm	inch or cm	inch		cm	inch or cm	inch
2·5	1	0·4		17·8	7	2·7
5·1	2	0·8		20	8	3·2
7·6	3	1·2		22·9	9	3·5
10·2	4	1·6		25·4	10	3·9
12·7	5	2·0		50·8	20	7·9
15·2	6	2·4		127	50	19·7

A rough way to convert from inches to cm: divide by 2 and multiply by 5; from cm to inches divide by 5 and multiply by 2.

metres – feet

m	ft or m	ft		m	ft or m	ft
0·3	1	3·3		2·4	8	26·3
0·6	2	6·6		2·7	9	29·5
0·9	3	9·8		3	10	32·8
1·2	4	13·1		6·1	20	65·6
1·5	5	16·4		15·2	50	164
1·8	6	19·7		30·5	100	328·1
2·1	7	23		304·8	1,000	3,280

A rough way to convert from ft to m: divide by 10 and multiply by 3; from m to ft divide by 3 and multiply by 10.

metres – yards

m	*yds or m*	yds		m	*yds or m*	yds
0·9	*1*	1·1		7·3	*8*	8·8
1·8	*2*	2·2		8·2	*9*	9·8
2·7	*3*	3·3		9·1	*10*	10·9
3·7	*4*	4·4		18·3	*20*	21·9
4·6	*5*	5·5		45·7	*50*	54·7
5·5	*6*	6·6		91·4	*100*	109·4
6·4	*7*	7·7		457·2	*500*	546·8

A rough way to convert from yds to m: subtract 10% from the number of yds; from m to yds add 10% to the number of metres.

LIQUID MEASURES

litres – gallons

litres	*galls or litres*	galls		litres	*galls or litres*	galls
4·6	*1*	0·2		36·4	*8*	1·8
9·1	*2*	0·4		40·9	*9*	2·0
13·6	*3*	0·7		45·5	*10*	2·2
18·2	*4*	0·9		90·9	*20*	4·4
22·7	*5*	1·1		136·4	*30*	6·6
27·3	*6*	1·3		181·8	*40*	8·8
31·8	*7*	1·5		227·3	*50*	11

1 pint = 0·6 litre 1 litre = 1·8 pint

A rough way to convert from galls to litres: divide by 2 and multiply by 9; from litres to galls divide by 9 and multiply by 2.

WEIGHT

kilogrammes – pounds

kg	*lb. or kg*	lb.		kg	*lb. or kg*	lb.
0·5	1	2·2		3·2	7	15·4
0·9	2	4·4		3·6	8	17·6
1·4	3	6·6		4·1	9	19·8
1·8	4	8·8		4·5	10	22·1
2·3	5	11·0		9·1	20	44·1
2·7	6	13·2		22·7	50	110·2

A rough way to convert from lb. to kg: divide by 11 and multiply by 5; from kg to lb. divide by 5 and multiply by 11.

grammes	oz.		oz.	grammes
100	3·5		2	57·1
250	8·8		4	114·3
500	17·6		8	228·6
1000 (1 kg)	35		16 (1 lb.)	457·2

TEMPERATURE

centigrade (°C)	fahrenheit (°F)
°C	°F
−10	14
−5	23
0	32
5	41
10	50
15	59
20	68
25	77
30	86
35	95
37	98·4
38	100·5
39	102
40	104
100	180

To convert °F to °C: deduct 32, divide by 9, multiply by 5; to convert °C to °F: divide by 5, multiply by 9 and add 32.

Vocabulary

Various groups of specialized words are given elsewhere in this book and these words are not usually repeated in the vocabulary:

A

a, an	ein/eine/ein	īne/īner/īne
able (to be)	können	kernen
about	ungefähr	ōōngefair
above	über	uiber
abroad	im Ausland	im **ows**lunt
accept (to)	annehmen	**un**-naymen
accident	der Unfall	**ōōn**ful
ache (to)	schmerzen	shmairtsen
acquaintance	der Bekannte	be**kun**ter
across	über, jenseits	uiber, **yaynzītes**
act (to)	handeln	hundeln
stage	spielen	shpeelen
add (to)	hinzufügen	hints**ōō**fuigen
address	die Adresse	ud**dress**er
admire (to)	bewundern	be**vōōn**dairn
admission	der Eintritt	**īne**-tritt
advice	der Rat	raht
aeroplane	das Flugzeug	**flōōk**tsoyg
afford (to)	sich leisten	zikh **līs**ten
afraid	ängstlich	**engst**likh
after	nach	nahkh
again	wieder	**vee**dair

against	gegen/wieder	gaygen/**vee**dair
age	das Alter	ulter
agree (to)	zustimmen	**tsōō**shtimmen
ahead	vorn	forn
air	die Luft	lōoft
air-conditioning	die Klimaanlage	**cleema-un**lahger
alike	ähnlich	**ayn**likh
all	alles	ulles
allow (to)	erlauben	air**low**ben
all right	in Ordnung	in **ord**nōong
almost	fast	fust
alone	allein	ul**līne**
along	entlang	ent**lung**
already	schon	shohn
also	auch	owkh
alter (to)	ändern	**en**dairn
alternative	die Alternative	ultairnah**teever**
although	obgleich	op**glīkh**
always	immer	immer
ambulance	der Krankenwagen	**crunken-vahgen**
America	Amerika	u**maireekah**
American *adj.*	amerikanisch	u**maireekahn**ish
noun	der Amerikaner	u**maireekahn**air
among	zwischen, bei	ts-**vish**en, bī

amuse (to)	amüsieren	umuizeeren
amusing	amüsant	umuizunt
ancient	sehr alt	zayr ult
and	und	ŏŏnt
angry	zornig	tsornikh
animal	das Tier	teer
anniversary	die Jahresfeier	yahresfī-er
annoyed	geärgert/verärgert	ge-airgert/fair-airgert
another	ein anderer	ine undairair
answer	die Antwort	untvort
answer (to)	antworten	untvorten
antique	die Antike	unteeker
antique shop	der Antiquitätenladen	unteekveetayten-lahden
any	irgendein	eergent-ine
anyone	irgendeiner	eergent-inair
anything	irgend etwas	eergent etvuss
anyway	jedenfalls	yayden-fuls
anywhere	irgendwo	eergent-voh
apartment	die Wohnung	vohnŏŏng
apologize (to)	sich entschuldigen	zikh entshŏŏldigen
appetite	der Appetit	uppeteet
appointment	die Verabredung	fairupraydŏŏng
architect	der Architekt	urkheetect
architecture	die Architektur	urkheetectŏŏr

area	das Gebiet	ge**beet**
arm	der Arm	urm
armchair	der Lehnstuhl	**layn**shtool
army	das Heer, die Armee	hayr, ar**may**
around	rings herum	rings hair**oom**
arrange (to)	festsetzen	**fest**zet-tsen
arrival	die Ankunft	**un**koonft
arrive (to)	ankommen	**un**commen
art	die Kunst	koonst
art gallery	die Kunstgalerie	**koonst**-galairee
artist	der Künstler	**kuinst**lair
as	wie	vee
as much as	soviel wie	zoh**feel** vee
as soon as	sobald	zoh**bult**
as well/also	auch	owkh
ashtray	der Aschenbecher	**ush**en-bekher
ask (to)	fragen	**frah**gen
asleep	eingeschlafen	**ine**-geshlahfen
at	an/zu/bei/um	un/tsoo/bi/oom
at last	endlich	**ent**likh
at once	sofort	zoh**fort**
atmosphere	die Atmosphäre	utmohs**fairer**
attention	die Aufmerksamkeit	**owf**mairkzumkite
attractive	reizend	**rite**-sent

auction	die Auktion	owktsee**ohn**
audience	die Zuhörer	**tsōō**herrer
aunt	die Tante	**tun**ter
Australia	Australien	ows**trah**leeyen
Australian	australisch	ows**trah**lish
Austria	Österreich	**er**stairīkh
Austrian	österreichisch	**er**stairīkhish
author	der Schriftsteller/	**shrift**-shtellair/
	Autor	**ow**tor
available	vorhanden	for**hun**den
average	durchschnittlich	**dōōrkh**-shnitlikh
awake	wach	vukh
away	weg	vek
awful	schrecklich	**shrek**likh

B

baby	das Baby	**bay**bee
bachelor	der Junggeselle	**yōōng**-gezeler
back	zurück	tsōō**ruick**
bad	schlecht	shlekht
bag	die Tasche	**tush**er
baggage	das Gepäck	ge**peck**
bait	der Köder	**ker**der

balcony	der Balkon	**bulkohn**
ball *sport*	der Ball	bul
ballet	das Ballet	bulet
band *music*	die Kapelle	cupeller
bank	die Bank	bunk
bare	nackt	nukt
basket	der Korb	corp
bath	das Bad	baht
bathe (to)	baden	bahden
bathing cap	die Bademütze	**bah**der-muitser
bathing costume	der Badeanzug	**bah**der-untsōōk
bathing trunks	die Badehose	**bah**der-hohzer
bathroom	das Badezimmer	**bah**der-tsimmer
battery	die Batterie	butteree
bay	die Bucht	bōōkht
be (to)	sein	zine
beach	der Strand	shtrunt
beard	der Bart	bahrt
beautiful	schön	shern
because	weil	vile
become (to)	werden	**vair**den
bed	das Bett	bet
bedroom	das Schlafzimmer	**shlahf**-tsimmer
before	vor/bevor	for/be-for

begin (to)	beginnen	**begin**nen
beginning	der Anfang	**un**fung
behind	hinter	**hin**tair
believe (to)	glauben	glowben
bell	die Glocke	glocker
belong (to)	gehören	**geher**-ren
below	unter	ōōntair
belt	der Gürtel	**guir**tell
bench	die Bank	bunk
bend (to)	biegen	beegen
beneath	unter	ōōntair
berth	das Bett	bet
beside	neben	nayben
besides	ausserdem	owsair**daym**
best	das Beste	bester
bet	die Wette	vetter
better	besser	besser
between	zwischen	ts-**vishen**
bicycle	das Fahrrad	**fahr**raht
big	gross	grohs
bill	die Rechnung	**rekh**nōōng
binoculars	das Fernglas	fernglahs
bird	der Vogel	**foh**gell
birthday	der Geburtstag	gebōōrtstahg

bite (to)	beissen	bīsen
bitter	herb	herp
blanket	die Wolldecke	**voll**decker
bleed (to)	bluten	blōōten
blind	blind	bleent
blond	blond	blont
blood	das Blut	blōōt
blouse	die Bluse	blōōzer
blow (to)	blasen	blahzen
(on) board	an Bord	un bort
boarding house	die Pension	pens**yohn**
boat	das Boot, Schiff	boht, sheef
body	der Körper	**ker**per
bolt	der Türriegel	**tuir**-reegel
bone	der Knochen	**k-no**khen
book	das Buch	bōōkh
book (to)	buchen	**bōō**khen
boot	der Stiefel	shteefel
border	die Grenze	grentser
borrow (to)	borgen	borgen
both	beide	bīder
bottle	die Flasche	flusher
bottle opener	der Flaschenöffner	**flush**en-erfnair
bottom	der Boden	boh-den

bowl	die Schüssel	**shui**sel
box *container*	die Schachtel	**shukh**tel
theatre	die Loge	lohjer
box office	die Kasse	cusser
boy	der Junge	yŏonger
bracelet	das Armband	**urm**bunt
braces	der Hosenträger	**hohzen**-trayger
brain	das Gehirn	ge**heern**
branch	der Zweig	ts-vig
brand	die Marke	murker
brassière	der Büstenhalter	**buisten**-hultair
break (to)	brechen	brekhen
breakfast	das Frühstück	**frui**-shtuick
breathe (to)	atmen	ahtmen
bridge	die Brücke	bruicker
briefs	der Schlüpfer	**shluip**fair
bright	leuchtend/hell	**loykh**tent/hell
bring (to)	bringen	bringen
British	britisch	british
broken	gebrochen/	ge**bro**khen/
	zerbrochen	tsair-**bro**khen
brooch	die Brosche	brosher
brother	der Bruder	**brŏo**der
bruise (to)	quetschen	**kvet**shen

brush	die Bürste	buirster
brush (to)	bürsten	buirsten
bucket	der Eimer	īmer
buckle	die Schnalle	shnuller
build (to)	bauen	bowen
building	das Gebäude	geboyder
bundle	das Bündel	buindel
burn (to)	brennen	brennen
burst (to)	bersten	bairsten
bus	der Bus	bōōs
bus stop	die Bushaltestelle	bōōs-hulter-shteller
business	das Geschäft	gesheft
busy	beschäftigt	besheftikht
but	aber	ahbair
button	der Knopf	k-nopf
buy (to)	kaufen	cowfen
by	von/bei	fon/bī

C

cabin	die Kabine	cubeener
call *telephone*	der Anruf	unrōōf
visit	der Besuch	bezōōkh

call (to) *summon*	rufen	rōōfen
name	nennen	nennen
telephone	anrufen	**un**rōōfen
visit	besuchen	bezōōkhen
calm	ruhig	rōō-eekh
camera	die Kamera/	**cu**mairuh/
	der Fotoapparat	**foto**-upp-ur-**aht**
camp (to)	zelten	tselten
camp site	der Zeltplatz	**tselt**-pluts
can (to be able)	können	kernen
can *tin*	die Dose	dozer
Canada	Kanada	**cu**nahdah
Canadian	kanadisch	**cu**nahdish
cancel (to)	abbestellen	**up**-beshtellen
candle	die Kerze	kairtser
canoe	das Kanu	**kah**noh
cap	die Mütze	muitser
capable	fähig	**fayh**-eekh
capital city	die Hauptstadt	**howpt**-shtuht
car	das Auto	**owt**oh
car park	der Parkplatz	**purk**pluts
caravan	der Wohnwagen	**vohn**vahgen
card	die Karte	curter
care (to)	sorgen	zorgen

careful	sorgsam	**zorg**zahm
careless	unachtsam	**ōōn**ukhtzahm
carry (to)	tragen	**trah**gen
cash	das Bargeld	**bahr**gelt
cash (to)	einlösen	**ine**-lerzen
cashier	der Kassierer	cuss**eer**air
casino	das Kasino	cuss**een**oh
castle	das Schloss/die Burg	shloss/**bōōrg**
cat	die Katze	**cut**ser
catalogue	der Katalog	cutu**lohg**
catch (to)	fangen	**fung**en
cathedral	der Dom	dohm
catholic	katholisch	cut**ohleésh**
cause	der Grund	groont
cave	die Höhle	**her**ler
central	zentral	tsen**trahl**
centre	das Zentrum	**tsen**trōōm
century	das Jahrhundert	yahr-**hōōn**dairt
ceremony	die Zeremonie	tsayremoh**nee**
certain	sicher	**zeek**hair
certainly	gewiss	ge**viss**
chair	der Stuhl	shtōōl
chambermaid	das Zimmermädchen	**tsimm**er-maytkhen
chance	die Möglichkeit	**merg**leekhkite

(by) chance	(durch) Zufall	**tsoo**ful
(small) change	das Kleingeld	**clīne**-gelt
change (to)	einwechseln	**īne**-veckzeln
charge	der Preis	price
charge (to)	berechnen	be**rekh**nen
cheap	billig	billikh
check (to)	nachrechnen	**nukh**-rekhnen
cheque	der Scheck	sheck
child	das Kind	keent
china	das Porzellan	portse**lahn**
choice	die Wahl	vahl
choose (to)	(aus)wählen	(**ows**)vaylen
church	die Kirche	keerkher
cigarette case	das Zigarettenetui	tseegah**retten**-aytvee
cine camera	die Filmkamera	**film**cumairuh
cinema	das Kino	**keen**oh
circus	der Zirkus	**tseer**kōos
city	die (Gross)stadt	(**grohs**)shtut
class	die Klasse	clusser
clean	rein	rīne
clean (to)	reinigen	**rīne**-eegen
clear	klar	klahr
clerk	der Beamte	be**umter**
cliff	die Klippe	clipper

climb (to)	besteigen	beshtīgen
cloakroom	die Toilette	twulette
clock	die Uhr	ōōr
close (to)	schliessen	shleesen
closed	geschlossen	geshlossen
cloth	der Stoff	shtof
clothes	die Kleider	klidair
cloud	die Wolke	volker
coach	der Autobus	owtohbŏŏs
coast	die Küste	cuister
coat	der Mantel	muntell
coathanger	der (Kleider)bügel	(klidair)buigel
coin	die Münze	muintser
cold	kalt	cult
collar	der Kragen	crahgen
collar stud	der Kragenknopf	crahgen k-nopf
collect (to)	sammeln	zummeln
colour	die Farbe	furber
comb	der Kamm	cum
come (to)	kommen	commen
come in (to)	hereinkommen	hairīne-commen
comfortable	bequem	bekvaym
common	allgemein	ulgemīne
company	die Gesellschaft	gezelshuft

compartment	das Abteil	uptile
complain (to)	sich beschweren	zikh beshvairen
complaint	die Beschwerde	beshvairder
complete	komplett	komplet
completely	ganz	gunts
concert	das Konzert	contsert
condition	der Zustand	tsooshtunt
conductor *bus*	der Schaffner	shuffnair
orchestra	der Dirigent	deereegent
congratulations	herzlichen Glückwunsch	hairtsleekhen gluikwoönsh
connect (to)	verbinden	fairbinden
connection *train, etc.*	der Anschluss	unshlooss
consul	der Konsul	conzool
consulate	das Konsulat	consoolaht
contain (to)	enthalten	enthulten
convenient	günstig	guinstikh
conversation	die Unterhaltung	oöntairhultoöng
cook	der Koch, die Köchin	kokh, kerkhin
cook (to)	kochen	kokhen
cool	kühl	kuil
copy	das Exemplar; die Kopie	eksemplahr; kohpee
copy (to)	kopieren	kohpeeyairen

cork	der Korken	corken
corkscrew	der Korkenzieher	**cork**en-tseeyer
corner	die Ecke	ecker
correct	richtig	**reekh**tikh
corridor	der Korridor	corree**dohr**
cosmetics	die Kosmetikartikel	cosme**teek**-artikell
cost	der Preis	price
cost (to)	kosten	costen
cotton	die Baumwolle	**bowm**voller
cotton wool	die Watte	vutter
couchette	der Liegeplatz	**leeger**-pluts
count (to)	zählen	**tsaylen**
country	das Land	lunt
couple	das Paar	pahr
course *dish*	das Gericht	ge**reekht**
courtyard	der Hof	hohf
cousin	der Vetter	fet-air
	die Kusine	cōō**zeener**
cover	die Decke	decker
cover (to)	bedecken	be**decken**
cow	die Kuh	koo
crease	die Falte	fulter
credit	das Guthaben	**goot**-hahben
	der Kredit	kray**deet**

crew	die Besatzung	besutsŏŏng
cross	das Kreuz	croyts
cross (to)	hinübergehen	hinuibair-gayen
crossroads	die Kreuzung	**croyts**-ŏŏng
crowd	die Menge	menger
crowded	voll	fol
cry (to)	schreien	shrī-yen
cufflinks	die Manschetten Knöpfe	munshetten **k-nerp**fer
cup	die Tasse	tusser
cupboard	der Schrank	shrunk
cure (to)	heilen	hilen
curious	neugierig	**noy**geerig
curl	die Locke	locker
current	die Strömung	**shtrer**mŏŏng
curtain	der Vorhang	**for**hung
curve	die Kurve	koorver
cushion	das Kissen	kissen
customs	der Zoll	tsoll
customs officer	der Zollbeamte	**tsoll**-beumter
cut	der Schnitt	shnit
cut (to)	schneiden	shniden

D

daily	täglich	**tayg**likh
damaged	beschädigt	be**shay**dikht
damp	feucht	foykht
dance	der Tanz	tunts
danger	die Gefahr	ge**fahr**
dangerous	gefährlich	ge**fair**likh
dark	dunkel	**doo**nkel
date	das Datum	**dah**tōōm
(*appointment*)	die Verabredung	fairu**pray**dōōng
daughter	die Tochter	**tokh**ter
day	der Tag	tahg
dead	tot	toht
deaf	taub	towb
dear *expensive*	teuer	**toy**er
decide (to)	entscheiden	ent**shi**den
deck	das Deck	deck
deckchair	der Liegestuhl	**leeg**er-shtōōl
declare (to)	verzollen	fair**sol**len
	erklären	air**klay**ren
deep	tief	teef
delay	die Verzögerung	fair-**tser**gerōōng
deliver (to)	austragen	**ows**trahgen

delivery	die Austragung	**ow**strahgōōng
demi-pension	das Zimmer mit halber Verpflegung	tsimmer mit hulbair fair**flay**gōōng
dentist	der Zahnarzt	**tsahn**ahrtst
deodorant	das desodorierende Mittel/der Deodorant	**days**ohdo**ree**render mittel/dayodo**runt**
depart (to)	abfahren	**up**fahren
department	die Abteilung	up**tīle**-ōōng
department store	das Warenhaus	**vah**renhows
departure	die Abfahrt	**up**fahrt
dessert	der Nachtisch	**nah-kh**tish
detour	der Umweg	**ōōm**vayk
dial (to)	wählen	vaylen
diamond	der Diamant	deeah**munt**
dice	der Würfel	vuirfel
dictionary	das Wörterbuch	**vert**airbōōkh
diet	die Diät	dee-ayt
diet (to)	Diät halten	dee-ayt hulten
different	verschieden	fairsheeden
difficult	schwierig	shveerikh
dine (to)	speisen, essen	spīzen, essen
dining room	der Speisesaal	shp**ī**zerzahl
dinner	das Abendessen	**ah**bent-essen

direct	direkt	dee**rekt**
direction	die Richtung	**reekht**ōong
dirty	schmutzig	**shmōōt**sikh
disappointed	enttäuscht	ent-**toysht**
discotheque	Diskothek	diskoh**tayk**
discount	der Preisnachlass	**prīce**-nukhluss
dish	die Schüssel	**shui**sel
disinfectant	das Desinfiziermittel	daysinfeet**seer**mittel
distance	die Entfernung	ent**fairn**ōong
disturb (to)	stören	shter-ren
ditch	der Graben	**grah**ben
dive (to)	tauchen	**towkh**en
diving board	das Sprungbrett	**sprōōng**bret
divorced	geschieden	ge**sheed**en
do (to)	tun	tōōn
dock (to)	anlegen	**un**laygen
doctor	der Arzt	ahrtst
dog	der Hund	hōōnt
doll	die Puppe	**pōō**per
door	die Tür	tuir
double	doppelt	**dopp**elt
double bed	das Doppelbett	**dopp**ell-bet
double room	das Doppelzimmer	**dopp**ell-tsimmer
down	hinunter	hin**ōōn**tair

downstairs	unten	**ōō**nten
dozen	das Dutzend	**dōō**tsent
drawer	die Schublade	shōōb-lahder
dream	der Traum	trowm
dress	das Kleid	clite
dressing-gown	der Morgenrock	morgenrock
dressmaker	die Damenschneiderin	**dah**men-shnīderin
drink (to)	trinken	treenken
drinking water	das Trinkwasser	**treenk**vussair
drive (to)	fahren	fahren
driver	der Fahrer	fahrer
drop (to)	fallen lassen	fullen lussen
drunk	betrunken	betrōōnken
dry	trocken	trocken
during	während	**vay**rent

E

each	jeder, e, es	yaydair, yayder, yaydes
early	früh	frui
earrings	die Ohrringe	**ohr**-ringer
east	der Osten	osten
easy	leicht	līkht
eat (to)	essen	essen

edge	der Rand	runt
eiderdown	das Federbett	fayderbet
elastic	das Gummiband	**gōo**meebunt
electric light bulb	die Glühbirne	**glui**beerner
electric point	die Steckdose	**shteck**doser
electricity	die Elektrizität	aylektreetsi**tayt**
elevator	der Fahrstuhl	**fahr**-shtōōl
embarrass (to)	in Verlegenheit setzen	in fair**layg**enhite zetsen
embassy	die Botschaft	**boht**shuft
emergency exit	der Notausgang	**noht**-owsgung
empty	leer	layr
end	das Ende	ender
engaged *people*	verlobt	fair**lohbt**
telephone	besetzt	be**zetst**
engine	der Motor	moh**tor**
England	England	**eng**lunt
English	englisch	**eng**lish
Englishman	der Engländer	**eng**lendair
enjoy (to)	geniessen	ge**nee**ssen
enough	genug	ge**nōōg**
enquiries	die Auskunft	**ows**kōōnft
enter (to)	hineintreten	hin**ine**-trayten
entrance	der Eingang	**ine**-gung

envelope	der (Brief)umschlag	(breef)ōōmshlahg
equipment	die Ausrüstung	ows-ruistōōng
escape (to)	entkommen	entcommen
Europe	Europa	oyrohpah
even *not odd*	gerade	gerahder
event	der Vorfall	forful
ever	immer	immer
every	jeder, e, es	yaydair, yayder, yaydes
everybody	jedermann	yaydairmun
everything	alles	ulles
everywhere	überall	uiberul
example	das Beispiel	bīshpeel
excellent	ausgezeichnet	owsgetsīkhnet
except	ausser	owssair
excess	das Übermass	uibermahss
exchange bureau	die Wechselstube	veckselshtōōber
exchange rate	der Wechselkurs	veckselkoors
excursion	der Ausflug	owsflōōg
excuse	die Entschuldigung	entshōōldeegōōng
exhausted	erschöpft	airsherpft
exhibition	die Ausstellung	owsshtellōōng
exit	der Ausgang	owsgung
expect (to)	erwarten	airvurten
expensive	teuer	toyer

explain (to)	erklären	**air**klayren
express	die Eilpost	**ī**le-post
express train	der Schnellzug	**shnel**tsōōg
extra	zusätzlich	**tsōō**zetslikh

F

fabric	der Stoff	shtof
face	das Gesicht	ge**zeekht**
face cream	die Gesichtskreme	ge**zeekhts**-craym
face powder	der (Gesichts) Puder	(ge**zeekhts**) pōōdair
fact	die Tatsache	**taht**zukher
factory	die Fabrik	fu**breek**
fade (to)	verblassen	fair**blussen**
faint (to)	in Ohnmacht fallen	in **ohn**mukht fullen
fair	blond	blont
fête	der Jahrmarkt	**yahr**murkt
fall (to)	fallen	**fullen**
family	die Familie	fu**meeleeyer**
far	weit	vīte
fare	das Fahrgeld	**fahr**gelt
farm	der Bauernhof	**bower**nhohf
farmer	der Bauer	**bower**
farther	weiter	**vīte**-air

fashion	die Mode	mohder
fast	schnell	shnell
fat	dick	dick
father	der Vater	fahtair
fault	der Fehler	fayler
fear	die Angst	ungst
feed (to)	ernähren	airnayren
feel (to)	fühlen	fuilen
female *adj.*	weiblich	**vipe**-likh
ferry	die Fähre	fairer
fetch (to)	holen	hohlen
few	wenig	**vay**nig
fiancé(e)	der/die Verlobte	fair**lohb**ter
field	das Feld	felt
fight (to)	kämpfen	kaimpfen
fill (to)	füllen	fuillen
film	der Film	film
find (to)	finden	feenden
fine	die Geldstrafe	**gelt**-shtrahfer
finish (to)	vollenden	follenden
finished	fertig	**fair**tikh
fire	das Feuer	**foyer**
fire escape	der Notausgang	**noht**-owsgung
first	erste	airster

first-aid	die erste Hilfe	airster heelfer
first class	die erste Klasse	airster clusser
fish	der Fisch	fish
fish (to)	angeln	**un**geln
fisherman	der Fischer	fisher
fishing tackle	die Angelgeräte	**un**gell-gerayter
fit	fähig	fayh-eekh
fit (to)	passen	pussen
flag	die Fahne	fahner
flat *adj.*	flach	flukh
noun	die Wohnung	**voh**nŏŏng
flight	der Flug	flŏŏg
flippers	Schwimmflossen	**shvim**flossen
float (to)	obenauf schwimmen	ohbe**nowf** shvimme
flood	die Flut	flŏŏt
floor	der Fussboden	**fŏŏs**-bohden
storey	der Stock	shtock
floor show	das Kabarett	cubu**rett**
flower	die Blume	blŏŏmer
fly	die Fliege	fleeger
fly (to)	fliegen	fleegen
fog	der Nebel	naybel
fold (to)	falten	fulten
follow (to)	folgen	folgen

food	das Essen	essen
foot	der Fuss	fŏŏs
football	der Fussball	**fŏŏs**bul
footpath	der Fussweg	**fŏŏs**-vayg
for	für	fuir
foreign	fremd	fremt
forest	der Wald	vult
forget (to)	vergessen	fair**gessen**
fork	die Gabel	**gah**bel
forward	vorwärts	**for**vairts
forward (to)	nachschicken	**nukh**shicken
fountain	der (Spring)brunnen	(**shpring**)brŏŏnen
fragile	zerbrechlich	tsair**brekh**likh
free	frei	frī
freight	die Fracht	frukht
fresh	frisch	frish
fresh water	das Süsswasser	**zuis**-vussair
friend	der Freund, die Freundin	froynt, **froyn**din
friendly	freundlich	**froynt**likh
from	von	fon
front	die Vorderseite	**for**derzīter
frontier	die Grenze	grentser
frozen	gefroren	ge**frohren**

fruit	die Frucht	frōōkht
full	voll	foll
fun	der Spass	shpahs
funny	komisch	**koh**mish
fur	der Pelz	pelts
furniture	die Möbel, der Hausrat	merbel, howsraht

G

gallery	die Galerie	gullai**ree**
gamble (to)	(um Geld) spielen	(ōōm **gelt**) shpeelen
game	das Spiel	shpeel
garage	die Garage	gu**rah**jer
garbage	der Abfall	**up**ful
garden	der Garten	gurten
gas	das Gas	gahs
gate	das Tor	tohr
gentlemen	Herren/ Männer	hairren/ mainner
German *adj.*	deutsch	doytsh
noun	der Deutsche	doytsher
Germany	Deutschland	**doytsh**lunt
get (to)	bekommen	becommen

get off (to)	aussteigen	**ows**-shtigen
get on (to)	einsteigen	**ine**-shtigen
gift	das Geschenk	ge**shaink**
girdle	der Hüftgürtel	**huift**-guirtell
girl	das Mädchen	**maydk**hen
give (to)	geben	**gayben**
glad	froh	froh
glass	das Glas	glahs
glasses	die Brille	**breeler**
gloomy	dunkel, schwermütig	**dōōn**kell, **shvair**muitikh
glorious	herrlich	**hair**likh
glove	der Handschuh	**hunt**shōō
go (to)	gehen	**gayen**
goal	das Ziel	tseel
goal (to score a)	ein Tor schiessen	tohr **sheessen**
god	Gott	got
gold	das Gold	gohlt
good	gut	gōōt
government	die Regierung	regee**rōōng**
granddaughter	die Enkelin	**en**kellin
grandfather	der Grossvater	**grohs**-fahtair
grandmother	die Grossmutter	**grohs**-mōōttair
grandson	der Enkel	**en**kel

grass	das Gras	grahs
grateful	dankbar	**dunk**bahr
gravel	der Kies	kees
great	gross	grohs
groceries	die Lebensmittel	**lay**bensmittel
ground	der Grund, der Boden	gröont, bohden
grow (to)	wachsen	vukhsen
guarantee	die Garantie	guran**tee**
guard	der Schaffner	**shuff**nair
guest	der Gast	gust
guide, guide book	der Führer	fuirer

H

hail	der Hagel	hahgel
hair	das Haar	hahr
hair brush	die Haarbürste	**hahr**-buirster
hairgrip	die Haarklammer	**hahr**clummer
hairpin	die Haarnadel	**hahr**nahdell
half	halb	hulp
half fare	der halbe Preis	hulber price
hammer	der Hammer	hummer
hand	die Hand	hunt
handbag	die Handtasche	**hunt**-tusher

handkerchief	das Taschentuch	**tush**entōōkh
hang (to)	hängen	haingen
happen (to)	geschehen	**ge**shayen
happy	glücklich	**glui**klikh
happy birthday	viel Glück	feel **gluik**
	zum Geburtstag	tsōōm ge**bōōrt**stahg
harbour	der Hafen	**hahf**en
hard	hart	hurt
difficult	schwierig	**shveer**ikh
hardly	kaum	kowm
hat	der Hut	hōōt
have (to)	haben	**hahb**en
he	er	air
health	die Gesundheit	ge**zōōnt**-hite
hear (to)	hören	**her**-ren
heart	das Herz	hairts
heat	die Hitze	**hit**ser
heating	die Heizung	**hī**tsōōng
heavy	schwer	shvair
heel *shoe*	der Absatz	**up**zuts
height	die Höhe	**her**-er
help	die Hilfe	**heel**fer
help (to)	helfen	**helf**en
hem	der Saum	zowm

her	sie, ihr, ihre	zee, eer, eerer
here	hier	heer
hers	ihr	eer
high	hoch	hohkh
hike (to)	wandern	**vun**dairn
hill	der Hügel, Berg	huigel, bairg
him	ihn, ihm	een, eem
hire (to)	mieten	meeten
his	sein/seine	zīne/zīner
hitch hike (to)	per Anhalter fahren	pair **un**hultair fahren
hold (to)	(fest)halten	(**fest**)hulten
hole	das Loch	lokh
holiday	der Feiertag	**fī**yairtahg
holidays	die Ferien	**fay**ree-en
hollow	hohl	hole
(at) home	zu Hause	tsoo **how**zer
honeymoon	die Hochzeitsreise	**hokh**-tsīts-rizer
hope	die Hoffnung	**hof**nŏŏng
hope (to)	hoffen	hoffen
horse	das Pferd	pfayrt
horse races	das Pferderennen	**pfayr**der-rennen
horse riding	das (Pferde)reiten	(**pfayrde**)rīten
hospital	das Krankenhaus	**crunk**enhows
host	der Gastgeber	**gust**gayber

hostess	die Gastgeberin	**gust**gayberin
hot	heiss	**h**is
hotel	das Hotel	hoh**tel**
hotel keeper	der Hotelier	hohte**leer**
hot water bottle	die Wärmflasche	**vairm**flusher
hour	die Stunde	**sht**o͞onder
house	das Haus	hows
how?	wie?	vee
how much, many?	wie viel, wie viele?	vee feel, vee feeler
hungry	hungrig	**h**o͞ongrikh
hurry (to)	eilen	**il**en
hurt (to)	schmerzen/	**shmairts**en/
	weh tun	vay to͞on
husband	der Mann, Gatte	mun, gutter

I

I	ich	eekh
if	wenn	ven
immediately	sofort	soh**fort**
important	wichtig	**veekh**tikh
in	in	in
include (to)	einschliessen	**ine**-shleessen
included	einbegriffen	**ine**-begriffen

inconvenient	ungelegen	**ŏŏn**gelaygen
incorrect	unrichtig, falsch	**ŏŏn**reekhtikh, fulsh
indeed	tatsächlich	tahtsekhlikh
indoors	ins Haus	ins hows
information	die Auskunft	owskŏŏnft
information bureau	die Auskunftstelle	owskŏŏnft-shteller
ink	die Tinte	tinter
inn	das Gasthaus	**gus**thows
insect	das Insekt	**in**zekt
insect bite	der Insektenstich	**in**zekten-shtikh
insect repellant	das Insektenbekämpf- ungsmittel	**in**zekten-be**kempf**- ŏŏngs-mittel
inside	drinnen	drinnen
instead of	statt	shtut
instructor	der Lehrer	**lay**rer
insurance	die Versicherung	fair-**zeek**hairŏŏng
insure (to)	versichern	fair-**zeek**hairn
interested	interessiert	intairess**eert**
interesting	interessant	intairess**unt**
interpreter	der Dolmetscher	**dol**metsher
into	in	in
introduce (to)	bekanntmachen	be**kunt**-mukhen
invitation	die Einladung	**ine**-lahdŏŏng
invite (to)	einladen	**ine**-lahden

Ireland	Irland	**eer**-lunt
Irish	irisch	**eer**ish
iron (to)	bügeln, plätten	**bui**geln, **plet**ten
island	die Insel	**een**zell
it	**es**	es

J

jacket	die Jacke	yucker
jar	der Krug/Topf	kroog/topf
jelly fish	die Qualle	kvuller
jewellery	der Schmuck	shmoock
job	die Stellung	shtelloong
journey	die Reise	rizer
jump (to)	springen	shpringen
jumper	der Pullover	poolohvair

K

keep (to)	halten, behalten	**hul**ten, be**hul**ten
key	der Schlüssel	**shlui**sel
kick (to)	(mit dem Fuss) stossen	mit dem foos shtohsen
kind (friendly)	freundlich	**froynt**likh

king	der König	kernikh
kiss	der Kuss	kōōs
kiss (to)	küssen	kuissen
kitchen	die Küche	kuikher
knickers	die Schlüpfer *pl.*	**shluip**fair
knife	das Messer	messair
knock (to)	klopfen	klopfen
know (to) *fact*	wissen	vissen
person	kennen	kennen

l

label	das Etikett	eteekett
lace	die Spitze	shpitser
ladies	Damen/Frauen	dahmen/frowen
lake	der See	zay
lamp	die Lampe	lumper
land	das Land	lunt
landing	die Landung	**lund**ōōng
landlord/lady	der Hauswirt/wirtin	**hows**veert/veertin
lane *town*	die Gasse	gusser
country	der Pfad	pfaht
language	die Sprache	shprahkher
large	**gross**	grohs

last	letzt	letst
late	spät	shpayt
laugh (to)	lachen	lukhen
lavatory	die Toilette	twuletter
lavatory paper	das Toilettenpapier	twuletten pupeer
law	das Gesetz	gezets
lead (to)	führen	fuiren
leaf	das Blatt	blut
leak (to)	auslaufen	**ows**lowfen
learn (to)	lernen	lairnen
least	mindest, wenigst	mindest, vaynikhst
(in the) least	am wenigsten	um **vay**nikhsten
leather	das Leder	**lay**der
leave (to) *abandon*	verlassen	fair**lus**sen
go away	abfahren	**up**fahren
(on the) left	links	leenks
left luggage	die Gepäckauf- bewahrung	gepeck-owf- bevahrŏong
lend (to)	leihen	lī-en
length	die Länge	lenger
less	weniger	**vay**nigair
lesson	der Unterricht	ŏŏnter-rikht
let (to) *rent*	vermieten	fair**mee**ten
allow	erlauben, lassen	airlowben, **lus**sen

letter	der Brief	breef
level crossing	der Bahnübergang	**bahn**uibergung
library	die Bibliothek	beeblee-oh**tayk**
licence	die Erlaubnis	air**lowb**nis
life	das Leben	**lay**ben
lift	der Fahrstuhl	**fahr**-shtool
light *colour*	hell	hell
weight	leicht	likht
noun	das Licht	likht
lighter	das Feuerzeug	**foy**air-tsoyg
lighter fuel	das Feuerzeug-Benzin	foyairtsoyg-bent**seen**
lighthouse	der Leuchtturm	**loykht**-toorm
like (to)	gern haben	gairn hahben
line	die Linie	**leenee**-yer
linen	das Leinen, die Bettwäsche	**li**nen, **bet**vesher
lingerie	die Unterwäsche	**oon**tervesher
lipstick	der Lippenstift	**lippen**-shtift
liquid *adj.*	flüssig	**flui**seekh
noun	die Flüssigkeit	**flui**seekh-kite
listen (to)	zuhören	**tsoo**her-ren
little	klein	kline
live (to)	leben	**lay**ben
loaf	das Brot	broht

local	lokal, hiesig, örtlich	**lohkahl, hee**seekh, **ert**likh
lock	das Schloss	shlos
lock (to)	schliessen	shleesen
long	lang	lung
look *at* (to)	ansehen	**un**zayen
for (to)	suchen	**zōō**khen
like (to)	aussehen	**ows**-zayen
loose	los(e)	lohs(er)
lorry	der Lastwagen	**lust**vahgen
lose (to)	verlieren	fair**leer**en
lost property office	das Fundbüro	**fōōnt**-buiroh
lot	viel	feel
loud	laut	lowt
love (to)	lieben	**lee**ben
lovely	schön	shern
low	niedrig	**need**reekh
luggage	das Gepäck	ge**peck**
(piece of) luggage	das Gepäckstück	ge**peck**shtuik
lunch	das Mittagessen	**mee**tahgessen

M

mad	verrückt	fair-**ruikt**
magazine	die Zeitschrift	**tsīte**-shrift
maid	das (Dienst)mädchen	(**deenst**)maydkhen
mail	die Post	post
main street	die Hauptstrasse	**howpt**strahser
make (to)	machen	mukhen
make-up	das Make-up	**may**kerp
male *adj.*	männlich	menlikh
man	der Mann	mun
manage (to)	auskommen	**ows**commen
manager	der Leiter	liter
manicure	die Maniküre	munee**kui**rer
many	viel(e)	feeler
map	die Karte	curter
market	der Markt	murkt
married	verheiratet	fairhī**rah**tet
Mass	die Messe	messer
massage	die Massage	mus**sah**jer
match	das Streichholz	**strīkh**-holts
sport	das Spiel	shpeel
material	der Stoff	shtof
matinée	die Matinee	mutee**nay**

mattress	die Matratze	mutruttser
me	mich, mir	meekh, meer
meal	die Mahlzeit	**mahl**tsite
measurements	die Masse	musser
meet (to)	treffen	treffen
mend (to)	reparieren	raypu**ree**ren
mess	die Unordnung	ŏŏnordnŏŏng
message	die Nachricht	**nakh**-riht
metal	das Metall	may**tahl**
middle	die Mitte	mitter
middle aged	in mittlerem Alter	in mitlerem ultair
middle class	die Mittelklasse	mittelclusser
mild	mild	milt
mine *pron.*	mein	mine
minute	die Minute	mee**nŏŏ**ter
mirror	der Spiegel	**shpee**gel
Miss	Fräulein	**froy**line
miss (to)	verpassen	fair**pus**sen
mistake	der Fehler	**fay**lair
mix (to)	(ver)mischen	(fair)**mish**en
mixed	gemischt	ge**misht**
modern	modern	moh**dairn**
moment	der Augenblick	**owg**en-blick
money	das Geld	gelt

month	der Monat	**moh**naht
monument	das Denkmal	**denk**mahl
moon	der Mond	mohnt
more	mehr	mayr
most	meist, die meisten	mīst, mīsten
mother	die Mutter	**mŏŏ**ttair
motor boat	das Motorboot	**moh**tor-boht
motor cycle	das Motorrad	**moh**tor-raht
motor racing	das Autorennen	**ow**toh-rennen
motorway	die Autobahn	**ow**tohbahn
mountain	der Berg	bairg
mouthwash	das Mundwasser	**mŏŏnt**vussair
Mr	Herr	hair
Mrs	Frau	frow
much	viel	feel
museum	das Museum	**mŏŏzay**ŏŏm
music	die Musik	**mŏŏ**zeek
must (to have to)	müssen	muissen
my	mein, meine	mīne, mīner
myself	mich	meekh

N

nail	der Nagel	**nah**gel
nailbrush	die Nagelbürste	**nah**gel-buirster
nailfile	die Nagelfeile	**nah**gel-fīler
nail polish	der Nagellack	**nah**gel-luk
name	der Name	nahmer
napkin	die Serviette	zairvee**y**etter
nappy	die Windel	**vin**del
narrow	schmal	shmahl
near	in der Nähe von ...	in dair **nay**er fon ...
nearly	fast	fust
necessary	notwendig	**noht**vendikh
necklace	die (Hals)kette	(huls)ketter
need (to)	brauchen	browkhen
needle	die Nadel	nahdel
net	das Netz	nets
never	nie, niemals	nee, **nee**muls
new	neu	noy
news	die Nachrichten	**nukh**-rikhten
newspaper	die Zeitung	**tsī**tōōng
next	nächst	naikhst
nice	nett	net
night	die Nacht	nukht

nightclub	der Nachtklub	**nukht**-clōōb
nightdress	das Nachthemd	**nukht**-hemt
nobody	niemand	**nee**munt
noisy	lärmend	**lair**ment
none	keine, keinen	**ki**ner, **ki**nen
north	der Norden	**nor**den
not	nicht	neekht
(bank) note	der Geldschein	**gelt**shine
notebook	das Notizbuch	**noh**teets-bōōkh
nothing	nichts	neekhts
notice	die Notiz	**noh**teets
notice (to)	bemerken	be**mair**ken
novel	der Roman	**roh**mahn
now	jetzt	yetst
number	die Nummer/	**nōō**mmer/
	Zahl	tsahl
nylon	das Nylon	**nui**lon
nylons	die Nylonstrümpfe	**nui**lon-shtruimpfer

O

occasion	die Gelegenheit	ge**lay**genhīte
occupation	der Beruf	be**rōōf**
occupied	besetzt	be**zetst**

ocean	das Meer	mayr
odd *not even*	ungerade	**oon**gerahder
strange	sonderbar	**zon**dairbahr
of	von	fon
off	ab	up
offer	das Angebot	**un**geboht
offer (to)	anbieten	**un**beeten
office	das Büro	buiroh
officer, official	der Beamte	beumter
officer *milit.*	der Offizier	offitseer
official *adj.*	offiziell	offits**yel**
often	oft	oft
oily	fettig	fettikh
ointment	die Salbe	zulber
old	alt	ult
on	auf, an	owf, un
once	einmal	**ine**-mahl
only	nur	no͞or
open (to)	öffnen	erfnen
open *p.p.*	geöffnet	ge-**erf**net
opening	die Öffnung	**erf**noͤong
opera	die Oper	**oh**pair
opportunity	die Gelegenheit	gelaygen-hite
opposite	gegenüber liegend	gaygen-**ui**ber leegent

or	oder	ohder
orchestra	das Orchester	orkestair
order (to)	bestellen	beshtellen
ordinary	gewöhnlich	gevernlikh
other	ander	under
otherwise	sonst	zonst
ought	sollen	zollen
our/ours	unser	ŏŏnzer
out	aus	ows
out of order	ausser Betrieb	owssair betreep
outside	draussen	drowsen
over	über	uiber
finished	fertig, zu Ende	fairtikh, tsŏŏ ender
over there	da drüben	dah druiben
overcoat	der Überrock	uiber-rock
overnight	über Nacht	uiber nukht
owe (to)	schulden	shŏŏlden
owner	der Besitzer	bezit-tser

P

pack (to)	packen	pucken
packet	das Paket	puckayt
page	die Seite	ziter

paid	bezahlt	betsahlt
pain	der Schmerz	shmairts
paint (to)	malen	mahlen
painting	das Gemälde	gemaylder
pair	das Paar	pahr
palace	der Palast	pulust
pale	blass	blus
paper	das Papier	pupeer
parcel	das Paket	puckayt
park	der Park	purk
park (to)	parken	purken
part	der Teil	tile
party	die Gesellschaft	gezel-shuft
pass (to)	vorbeigehen	forbī-gayen
passenger	der Passagier	pussujeer
passport	der Pass	pus
past	vorig, früher	forikh, frui-air
path	der Pfad	pfaht
patient	der Patient	putsyent
pavement	der Fussteig	fōōs-shtig
pay (to)	bezahlen	betsahlen
peak	der Gipfel	geepfel
pearl	die Perle	pairler
pebble	der Kiesel	keesel

pedal	das Pedal	**pedahl**
pedestrian	der Fussgänger	**fōōs**genger
pen	die Feder	**fay**der
pencil	der Bleistift	**blī**shtift
penknife	das Federmesser	**fay**der-messer
people	die Leute	**loy**ter
perfect	tadellos	**tah**del-lohs
per (person)	pro (Person)	pro (pair**zohn**)
performance	die Aufführung	**owf**-fuirōōng
perfume	das Parfüm	pur**fuim**
perhaps	vielleicht	feel**īkht**
perishable	leicht verderblich	līkht fair**dair**blikh
permit	die Erlaubnis	air**lowb**nis
permit (to)	erlauben	air**low**ben
person	die Person	pair**zohn**
personal	persönlich	pair**zern**likh
petrol	das Benzin	bent**seen**
petrol station	die Tankstelle	**tunk**-shteller
petticoat	der Unterrock	**ōōn**ter-rock
photograph	die Photographie	phohtoh-gru**fee**
photographer	der Photograph	phohtoh-**gruf**
piano	das Klavier	clu**veer**
pick (to)	aussuchen	**ows**-zōōkhen
flowers	pflücken	**pflui**ken

picnic	das Picknick	**peek**-neek
piece	das Stück	shtuik
pier	die Landungsbrücke	**lund**ōōngs-bruiker
pillow	das Kopfkissen	**kopf**-kissen
pin	die Stecknadel	**shteck**-nahdel
(safety) pin	die Sicherheitsnadel	**zee**khairhites-nahdel
pipe	die Pfeife	pfīfer
place	der Ort	ort
plain	einfach	**īne**-fukh
plan	der Plan	plahn
plant	die Pflanze	pfluntser
plastic	plastik	**plus**teek
plate	der Teller	tellair
platform	der Bahnsteig	**bahn**-shtīg
play	das Schauspiel	**show**-shpeel
play (to)	spielen	shpeelen
player	der Spieler	shpeeler
please	bitte	bitter
plenty	die Menge	menger
pliers	die Zange *sing.*	tsunger
plug	der Stöpsel	**shterp**sel
electric	der Stecker	shteckair
pocket	die Tasche	tusher
point	der Punkt	pōōnkt

poisonous	giftig	giftikh
policeman	der Polizist	pohlee**tsist**
police station	die Polizeiwache	pohlee**tsī**-vukher
poor	arm	urm
popular	populär	pohpoo**lair**
port	der Hafen	hahfen
possible	möglich	**mer**glikh
post (to)	einstecken/aufgeben	**ine**-shtecken/**owf**-gayben
post box	der Briefkasten	**breef**-custen
postcard	die Postkarte	**post**-curter
postman	der Briefträger	**breef**-trayger
post office	die Post	post
postpone (to)	zurückstellen	tsoo**ruik**shtellen
pound	das Pfund	pfoont
powder	der Puder	p...
prefer (to)	vorziehen	**for**tseeyen
prepare (to)	vorbereiten	**for**beriten
present *gift*	das Geschenk	ge**shaink**
press (to)	bügeln, plätten	buigeln, pletten
pretty	hübsch	huipsh
price	der Preis	price
priest	der Priester	preestair
print	der (Ab)druck	(up)dro͞ock
print (to)	abdrucken	(up)dro͞ocken

private	privat/	pree**vaht**/
	persönlich	pair**zern**likh
problem	das Problem	pro**blaym**
profession	der Beruf	ber**oof**
programme	das Programm	proh**grum**
promise	das Versprechen	fair**shpre**khen
promise (to)	versprechen	fair**shpre**khen
prompt	sofortig	**zoh**fortikh
protestant	der Protestant	protes**tunt**
provide (to)	besorgen	be**zor**gen
public	öffentlich	**erf**entlikh
pull (to)	ziehen	**tsee**yen
pump	die Pumpe	**poom**per
pure	rein	**rine**
purse	das Portemonnaie/	portmon**nay**/
	die Geldbörse	**gelt**berrser
push (to)	stossen	**shtoh**ssen
put (to)	stellen	**shtel**len
pyjamas	der Schlafanzug	**shlahf**-unts**oog**

Q

| quality | die Qualität | k-vulee**tayt** |
| quantity | die Quantität | k-vuntee**tayt** |

quarter	das Viertel	feertel
queen	die Königin	**ker**neegin
question	die Frage	frahger
queue	die Schlange	shlunger
queue (to)	Schlange stehen	shlunger shtayen
quick(ly)	schnell	shnel
quiet(ly)	ruhig	rōō-ikh
quite	ganz	gunts

R

race	das Rennen	rennen
racecourse	die Rennbahn	**renn**bahn
radiator	der Heizkörper	**hīts**-kerper
radio	das Radio	**rah**deeyoh
railway	die Eisenbahn	**ī**zen-bahn
rain	der Regen	raygen
rain (to)	regnen	raygnen
raincoat	der Regenmantel	**ray**gen-muntel
rare	rar	rahr
rather	ziemlich	tseemlikh
raw	roh	roh
razor	der Rasierapparat	**ruzeer** upuraht
razor blade	die Rasierklinge	**ruzeer**-clinger

reach (to)	reichen	rīkhen
read (to)	lesen	layzen
ready	bereit	berīte
real	wahr	vahr
really	wirklich	**veer**klikh
reason	der Grund	grŏŏnt
receipt	die Quittung	**k**-veetŏŏng
receive (to)	bekommen	be**comm**en
recent	neu	noy
recipe	das Rezept	re**tsept**
recognize (to)	erkennen	air**kenn**en
recommend (to)	empfehlen	emp**fayl**en
record	die Schallplatte	**shul**plutter
record *sport*	der Rekord	**record**
refreshments	die Erfrischungen	air**frish**ŏŏngen
refrigerator	der Kühlschrank	**cuil**shrunk
regards	die Grüsse	**gruiss**er
register (to)	(Gepäck) aufgeben, einschreiben	(ge**peck**) **owf**gayben, īne-shrīben
relative	der Verwandter, die Verwandte	fair**vund**tair, fair**vund**ter
religion	die Religion	rayligy**ohn**
remember (to)	sich erinnern	zikh air**inn**airn
rent	die Miete	**meet**er
rent (to)	mieten, leihen	**meet**en, lī-en

repair (to)	reparieren	repahreeren
repeat (to)	wiederholen	**vee**derhohlen
reply (to)	antworten	**unt**vorten
reservation	die Reservierung	rezairveeröóng
reserve (to)	reservieren	rezairveeren
reserved	reserviert	rezairveert
restaurant	das Restaurant	restorunt
restaurant car	der Speisewagen	**shp**yzer-vahgen
return (to)	zurückkehren	tsööruik-kairen
return (to) *give back*	zurückgeben	tsööruik-gayben
reward	die Belohnung	belohnöóng
ribbon	das Band	bunt
rich	reich	rīkh
ride	die Fahrt	fahrt
ride (to)	reiten	rīten
right *opp. left*	rechts	rekhts
right *opp. wrong*	richtig	**reekh**tikh
ring	der Ring	ring
ripe	reif	rīfe
rise (to)	sich erheben	zikh airhayben
rise (to) *get up*	aufstehen	**owf**shtayen
river	der Fluss	flöós
road	die Strasse	strahser
rock	der Felsen	felzen

roll (to)	rollen	rollen
roller *hair*	der Lockenwickler	**lock**enwiclair
roof	das Dach	dukh
room	das Zimmer	tsimmer
rope	das Seil	zíle
rotten	faul	fowl
rough	rauh, grob	row, grohp
round	rund	roȯnt
rowing boat	das Ruderboot	**roȯ**der-boht
rubber	das Gummi	goȯmee
rubbish	der Abfall	**up**ful
rucksack	der Rucksack	**roȯk**zuk
rude	unverschämt	**oȯn**fairshaymt
ruin	die Ruine	roȯeener
rule (to)	beherrschen	be**hair**shen
run (to)	laufen	lowfen

S

sad	traurig	**trow**reekh
safe	sicher	zeekhair
sailor(s)	der Seeman (die Seeleute)	**zay**mun (**zay**loyter)
sale *clearance*	der Ausverkauf	**ows**fairkowf

(for) sale	verkäuflich	fair**koyf**likh
salesgirl	die Verkäuferin	fair**koyf**erin
salesman	der Verkäufer	fair**koyf**er
salt water	das Salzwasser	**zults**-vussair
same	der-, die-, das selbe	**zelber**
sand	der Sand	zunt
sandal	die Sandale	sund**ahler**
sanitary towel	die Binde	binder
satisfactory	befriedigend	be**free**digent
saucer	die Untertasse	ōōntertusser
save (to)	retten	retten
say (to)	sagen	zahgen
scald (to)	verbrühen	fair**bruien**
scarf	der Schal	shahl
scenery	die Landschaft	**lund**shuft
scent	das Parfüm	pur**fuim**
school	die Schule	shōōler
scissors	die Schere	shairer
Scotland	Schottland	**shot**lunt
Scottish	schottisch	**shottish**
scratch (to)	kratzen	krutsen
screw	die Schraube	shrowber
screwdriver	der Schraubenzieher	**shrow**bentsee-er
sculpture	die Skulptur	skōōlpt**ōōr**

sea	das Meer/die See	mayr/zay
sea food	die Meeresfrüchte	**mayr**es-fruikhter
seasickness	die Seekrankheit	**zay**-krunkhite
season	die Jahreszeit	**yahr**es-tsite
seat	der Platz	pluts
second	zweite	ts-viter
see (to)	sehen	zayen
seem (to)	scheinen	shinen
sell (to)	verkaufen	fair**kow**fen
send (to)	schicken	shicken
separate	getrennt	ge**trent**
serious	ernst	airnst
serve (to)	bedienen	bedeenen
served	serviert	zair**veert**
service	die Bedienung	bedeenööng
service *church*	der Gottesdienst	**got**tesdeenst
several	mehrere	**mayr**erer
sew (to)	nähen	nayen
shade *colour*	der Farbton	**furp**tohn
shade/shadow	der Schatten	shutten
shallow	flach	flukh
shampoo	das Schampoo	shum**poo**
shape	die Form	form
share (to)	teilen	tilen

sharp	scharf	shurf
shave (to)	rasieren	rahzeeren
shaving brush	der Rasierpinsel	rahzeer-pinzel
shaving cream	die Rasiercreme	rahzeer-craymer
she	sie	zee
sheet	das Bettlaken	betlahken
shell	die Muschel	mōōshell
shelter	das Obdach	opdukh
shine (to)	scheinen	shīnen
shingle	der Kiesel	keezel
ship	das Schiff	sheef
shipping line	die Schiff-fahrts-gesellschaft	sheef-fahrts-gezelshuft
shirt	das Hemd	hemt
shock	der Stoss	shtohs
shoe	der Schuh	shōō
shoelace	der Schnürsenkel	shnuir-zenkel
shoe polish	die Schuhwichse	shōōvigser
shop	der Laden/ das Geschäft	lahden/ gesheft
shopping centre	das Einkaufszentrum	īne-kowfs-tsentrōōm
shore	das Ufer, die Küste	ōōfair, kuister
short	kurz	kōōrts
shorts	die Shorts	shorts

show	die Vorstellung	**for**shtelloong
show (to)	zeigen	tsigen
shower	die Dusche	dōōsher
shut (to)	schliessen	shleesen
shut *p.p.*	geschlossen	ge**shlossen**
side	die Seite	ziter
sights	die Sehenswürdig- keiten	**say**ens-vuirdikh-**kī**ten
sightseeing	die Besichtigung von Sehenswürdig- keiten	be**zikh**tigōōng von **say**ens-vuirdikh- **kī**ten
sign	das Zeichen	tsikhen
sign (to)	unterschreiben	ōōntair-**shrī**ben
signpost	der Wegweiser	**vayk**-vizer
silver	das Silber	zilbair
simple	einfach	īne-fukh
since	seit	zite
sing (to)	singen	zingen
single	einzig, einzeln	**ī**ne-tsig, **ī**ne-tseln
single room	das Einzelzimmer	**ī**ne-tsel-tsimmer
sister	die Schwester	shvester
sit (to)	sitzen	zitsen
sit down (to)	sich setzen	zikh zetsen
size	die Grösse	grerser

skating	das Schlittschuh-laufen	**shlit**shōō-lowfen
skid (to)	rutschen	rōōtshen
skiing	das Skilaufen	**shee**-lowfen
skirt	der Rock	rock
sky	der Himmel	himmel
sleep (to)	schlafen	shlahfen
sleeper	der Schlafwagen	**shlahf**-vahgen
sleeping bag	der Schlafsack	**shlahf**-zuck
sleeve	der Ärmel	**air**mel
slice	die Schnitte	shnitter
slip	der Unterrock	**ōōn**ter-rock
slipper	der Hausschuh	**hows**-shōō
slowly	langsam	**lung**zum
small	klein	kline
smart	schick	shick
smell	der Geruch	ger**ōō**kh
smell (to)	riechen	reekhen
smile (to)	lächeln	lekheln
smoke (to)	rauchen	rowkhen
smoking compart-ment	Raucher	**row**khair
(no) smoking	rauchen (verboten)	rowkhen fair**boh**ten
snow	der Schnee	shnay

snow (to)	schneien	shni-yen
so	so	zoh
soap	die Seife	zifer
soap powder	das Seifenpulver	**zi**fenpoolfair
sober	nüchtern	**nuikh**tairn
sock	die Socke	zocker
soft	weich	vikh
sold	verkauft	fair**kowft**
sole *shoe*	die Sohle	zohler
solid	fest	fest
some	einige, etwas	**i**neeger, **etvus**
somebody	jemand	**yay**munt
somehow	irgendwie	**eer**gentvee
something	etwas	**etvus**
sometimes	manchmal	**munkh**mahl
somewhere	irgendwo	**eer**gentvoh
son	der Sohn	zohn
song	das Lied	leet
soon	bald	bult
sort	die Art	ahrt
sound	der Laut	lowt
sour	sauer	**zow**er
south	der Süden	zuiden
souvenir	das Andenken	**un**denken

space	der Raum	rowm
spanner	der Schrauben- schlüssel	**shrow**ben-shluissel
spare	Ersatz-, Reserve-	**air**zats, re**zair**ver
speak (to)	sprechen	shprekhen
speciality	die Spezialität	shpaytseeyuli**tayt**
spectacles	die Brille *sing.*	briller
speed	die Geschwindigkeit	ge**shvin**dikh-kīte
speed limit	die Geschwindigs- grenze	ge**shvin**dikhs-grentser
spend (to)	ausgeben	**ows**gayben
spoon	der Löffel	**ler**ffel
sport	der Sport	shport
sprain (to)	verstauchen	fair**shtow**khen
spring *water*	die Quelle	kveller
square	viereckig	feer-eckikh
square metre	das Quadratmeter	kvu**draht**maytair
square *noun*	der Platz	pluts
stable	der Stall	shtul
stage	die Bühne	buiner
stain	der Fleck	fleck
stained	beschmutzt	be**shmōōtst**
stairs	die Treppe	trepper
stale	schal	shahl
stalls	der Sperrsitz	**shpair**-zits

stamp	die Briefmarke	**breef**murker
stand (to)	stehen	shtayen
star	der Stern	shtairn
start (to)	anfangen	**un**fungen
(main) station	der (Haupt)bahnhof	(**howpt**)bahnhohf
statue	die Bildsäule	**beelt**-zoyler
stay (to)	bleiben	bliben
step	der Schritt	shrit
steward	der Steward	**shtōō**-urt
stewardess	die Stewardess	**shtōō**-urdess
stick	der Stock	shtock
stiff	starr	shtur
still *not moving*	still	shtil
still *time*	noch	nokh
sting	der Stich	steekh
stocking	der Strumpf	shtrōōmpf
stolen	gestohlen	geshtohlen
stone	der Stein	shtine
stool	der Stuhl, Hocker	shtōōl, hockair
stop (to)	(an)halten	(**un**)hulten
storm	der Sturm	shtōōrm
stove	der Ofen	ohfen
straight	gerade	gerahder
straight on	gerade aus	gerahder **ows**

strange	sonderbar	**zon**dairbahr
strap	der Riemen	**ree**men
stream	der Bach	bukh
street	die Strasse	**strah**ser
stretch (to)	(aus)strecken	(**ows**)shtrecken
string	die Schnur	shnoor
strong	stark	shturk
student	der Student	shtoo**dent**
stung (to be)	gestochen werden	geshto**khen** vairden
style	der Stil	shteel
suburb	der Vorort	**for**ort
subway	die Unterführung	**oo**nterfuiroong
such	solch	solkh
suede	das Wildleder	**vilt**-laydair
sugar	der Zucker	tsoocker
suggestion	der Vorschlag	**for**shlahg
suit *men*	der Anzug	**unt**soog
suit *women*	das Kostüm	cos**tuim**
suitcase	der (Hand)koffer	(hunt)coffer
sun	die Sonne	zonner
sunbathe (to)	sonnenbaden	**zon**nen-bahden
sunburn	der Sonnenbrand	**zon**nen-brunt
sunglasses	die Sonnenbrille	**zon**nen-briller
sunhat	der Sonnenhut	**zon**nen-hoot

sunny	sonnig	**zon**nikh
sunshade	der Sonnenschirm	**zon**nen-sheerm
suntan oil	das Sonnenöl	**zon**nen-erl
supper	das Abendessen	**ah**bent-essen
sure	sicher	zeekher
surgery	das Sprechzimmer	**shprekh**-tsimmer
surgery hours	die Sprechstunde	**shprekh**-stoonder
surprise	die Überraschung	uibair-**ru**shoong
surprise (to)	überraschen	uibair-**ru**shen
suspender belt	der Strumpfgürtel	**shtroompf**-guirtel
sweater	der Pullover	**poo**lohvair
sweet	süss	zuis
sweets	die Bonbons	bon**bons**
swell (to)	anschwellen	**un**shvellen
swim (to)	schwimmen	shvimmen
swimming pool	die Badeanstalt	**bah**der-unstult
swings	die Schaukel, die Wippe	showkel, vipper
Swiss	schweizerisch	**shvit**serish
switch *elec.*	der (Licht)schalter	(**likht**)shultair
Switzerland	Schweiz	shvits
swollen	angeschwollen	**un**geshvollen
synagogue	die Synagoge	**zu**inagohger

T

table	der Tisch	tish
tablecloth	das Tischtuch	**tish**tōōkh
tablet	die Tablette	**tub**letter
tailor	der Schneider	shnīdair
take (to)	nehmen	naymen
talk (to)	reden	rayden
tall	gross	grohs
tank	der Tank	tunk
tanned	sonnverbrannt	**zon**fairbrunt
tap	der Wasserhahn	**vus**sair-hahn
taste	schmecken	shmecken
tax	die (Kur)taxe	(cōōr)-tukser
taxi	das Taxi	**tuk**see
taxi rank	der Taxistand	**tuk**see-shtunt
teach (to)	lehren	layren
tear	der Riss	ris
tear (to)	(zer)reissen	(tsair)rissen
teaspoon	der Teelöffel	**tay**-lerffel
telegram	das Telegramm	tayle**grum**
telephone	das Telefon	tayle**fohn**
telephone (to)	telefonieren	taylefoh**neeren**
telephone box	die Telefonzelle	tayle**fohn**-tseller

telephone call	der Anruf	**un**rōōf
telephone directory	das Telefonbuch	tayle**fohn**-bōōkh
telephone number	die Telefonnummer	tayle**fohn**-nōōmmair
telephone operator	das Telefonfräulein	tayle**fohn**-froyline
television	das Fernsehen	**fairn**zayen
tell (to)	erzählen	airtsaylen
temperature	die Temperatur	tempairut**ōōr**
temple	der Tempel	tempel
temporary	vorläufig, vorübergehend	**for**loyfeekh, foru̇ibairgayent
tennis	das Tennis	**tennis**
tent	das Zelt	tselt
tent peg	der Zeltpflock	**tselt**-pflock
tent pole	der Zeltmast	**tselt**must
terrace	die Terrasse	tair**russ**er
than	als	uls
that	jener, e, es	yaynair, yayner, yaynes
the	der, die, das	dair, dee, dus
theatre	das Theater	tay**ah**tair
their(s)	ihr, ihre	eer, eerer
them	sie, ihnen	zee, eenen
then	dann	dun
there	da, dort	dah, dort

there is	es ist/gibt	es eest/geebt
there are	es sind/gibt	es zint/geebt
thermometer	das Thermometer	tairmoh**may**tair
these	diese	deezer
they	sie	zee
thick	dick	dick
thin	dünn	duin
thing	das Ding, die Sache	ding, zukher
think (to)	denken	denken
thirsty	durstig	dōōrstikh
this	dieser, e, es	deezair, deezer, deezes
those	jene	yayner
though	obwohl	op**vohl**
thread	der Faden	fahden
through	durch	dōōrkh
throughout	während	vairent
throw (to)	werfen	vairfen
thunderstorm	das Gewitter	gevittair
ticket	die Karte	curter
tide	die Gezeiten (*pl.*)	getsīten
tie	der Schlips	shlips
tie *sport*	der Gleichstand	**glīkh**-shtunt
tight	eng	eng
time	die Zeit	tsīt

timetable	der Fahrplan	**fahr**plahn
tin	die Dose	dohzer
tin opener	der Dosenöffner	**doh**zen-erfnair
tip	das Trinkgeld	**trink**gelt
tip (to)	ein Trinkgeld geben	ine **trink**gelt gayben
tired	müde	muider
tissues	die Papiertücher	pupeer-tuikhair
to	zu, nach	tsōō, nukh
tobacco	der Tabak	**tu**buck
tobacco pouch	der Tabaksbeutel	**tu**bucksboytel
together	zusammen	tsōō**zum**men
toilet	die Toilette	twu**let**ter
toilet paper	das Toilettenpapier	twu**let**tenpupeer
too *also*	auch	owkh
too (much, many)	zu (viel, viele)	tsōō (feel, feeler)
toothbrush	die Zahnbürste	**tsahn**-buirster
toothpaste	die Zahnpasta	**tsahn**-pustu
toothpick	der Zahnstocher	**tsahn**-shtokhair
top	das obere Ende	**oh**bairer ender
torch	die Taschenlampe	**tush**en-lumper
torn	zerrissen	tsair**ris**sen
touch (to)	berühren	be**ru**iren
tough	hart, zäh	hurt, tsay
tour	die (Rund)reise	(**rōōnt**)rizer

tourist	der Tourist	**tōō**reest
towards	gegen	gay-gen
towel	das Handtuch	**hunt**-tōōkh
tower	der Turm	**tōō**rm
town	die Stadt	shtut
town hall	das Rathaus	**rah**thows
toy	das Spielzeug	**shpeel**-tsoyg
traffic	der Verkehr	fair**kayr**
traffic jam	die Verkehrsstockung	fair**kayrs**-shtock**ōōng**
traffic lights	die Verkehrsampel	fair**kairs**-umpell
trailer	der Anhänger	**un**henger
train	der Zug	tsōōg
tram	die Strassenbahn,	**shtrah**senbahn,
	S-bahn	es-bahn
transfer (to)	übertragen	uiber**trah**gen
transfer (to) *travel*	umbuchen	**ōōm**bōōkhen
transit	der Durchgang	**dōō**rkhgang
translate (to)	übersetzen	uiber-**zetsen**
travel (to)	reisen	**ri**zen
travel agency	das Reisebüro	**ri**zer-buiroh
traveller	der Reisende	**ri**zendair
traveller's cheque	der Reisescheck	**ri**ze-sheck
treat (to)	behandeln	be**hund**eln
treatment	die Behandlung	be**hunt**lōōng

tree	der Baum	bowm
trip	der Ausflug	**ows**flōōg
trouble	die Mühe	mui-er
trousers	die Hose *sing.*	hohzer
true	wahr	vahr
trunk	der Koffer	coffair
trunks *swimming*	die Badehose	bahder-hohzer
truth	die Wahrheit	**vahr**hite
try (to)	versuchen	fairzōōkhen
try on (to)	anprobieren	**un**prohbeeren
tunnel	der Tunnel	**tōō**nel
turn (to)	umdrehen	**ōōm**drayen
turning	die Biegung	beegōōng
tweezers	die Pinzette *sing.*	pintsetter
twin-bedded room	das Zweibettzimmer	tsvībet-tsimmer
twisted	verrenkt	fairrenkt

U

ugly	hässlich	heslikh
umbrella	der Regenschirm	**ray**gensheerm
(beach) umbrella	der Sonnenschirm	**zon**nensheerm
uncle	der Onkel	onkel
uncomfortable	unbequem	**ōōn**bekvaym

under(neath)	unter	ŏŏntair
underground	die U-bahn	ŏŏ-bahn
understand (to)	verstehen	fair**shtayen**
underwater fishing	die Unterwasser-fischerei	ŏŏntairvusserfisher-ī
underwear	die Unterwäsche	ŏŏntair-vesher
university	die Universität	ŏŏneevairsee**tayt**
unpack (to)	auspacken	**ows**pucken
until	bis	bis
unusual	ungewöhnlich	ŏŏngevernlikh
up	auf	owf
upstairs	oben	ohben
urgent	dringend	dringent
us	uns	ŏŏns
U.S.A.	die Vereinigten Staaten	fairīnigter shtahten
use (to)	brauchen	browkhen
useful	brauchbar	**browkh**bahr
useless	unbrauchbar	ŏŏn**browkh**bahr
usual	gewöhnlich	ge**vern**likh

V

vacancies	Zimmer frei	**tsimm**er frī
vacant	frei	frī
vacation	die Ferien	**fai**reeyen
valid	gültig	**guil**tikh
valley	das Tal	tahl
valuable	wertvoll	**vairt**fol
value	der Wert	vairt
vase	die Vase	**vah**zer
vegetable	das Gemüse	ge**mui**zer
vegetarian	der Vegetarier	fege**tah**ree-er
ventilation	die Ventilation	ventilah**tsyohn**
very	sehr	zayr
very much	viel, sehr	feel, zayr
vest	das Unterhemd	**oon**tairhemt
view	der Blick	blik
villa	das Villa	**vee**lah
village	das Dorf	dorf
violin	die Geige	**gī**ger
visa	das Visum	**vee**zoom
visibility	die Sicht(barkeit)	**sikht**bahrkīte
visit	der Besuch	be**zookh**
visit (to)	besuchen	be**zook**hen

voice	die Stimme	shtimmer
voltage	die Spannung	**shpun**nŏŏng
voyage	die Reise	rizer

W

wait (to)	warten	**vur**ten
waiter	der Kellner	**kel**nair
waiting room	der Warteraum	**vur**ter-rowm
waitress	die Kellnerin	**kel**nerin
wake (to)	aufwachen	**owf**-vukhen
Wales	Wales	vayls
walk	der Spaziergang	shput**seer**-gung
walk (to)	spazierengehen	shput**seeren**-gayen
wall *inside*	die Wand	vunt
wall *outside*	die Mauer	mowair
wall plug	der Stecker	shteckair
wallet	die Brieftasche	**breef**-tusher
want (to)	wollen	vollen
wardrobe	der Kleiderschrank	**klī**der-shrunk
warm	warm	vurm
wash (to)	waschen	vushen
washbasin	das Waschbecken	**vush**-becken
waste	der Abfall	**up**ful

waste (to)	verschwenden	fair**shven**den
watch	die Armbanduhr	**urm**bunt-ōōr
water	das Wasser	vussair
waterfall	der Wasserfall	**vuss**airful
water skiing	das Wasserskilaufen	**vuss**air-shee-lowfen
waterproof	wasserdicht	**vuss**airdikht
wave	die Welle	veller
way	der Weg	vayg
we	wir	veer
wear (to)	tragen	trahgen
weather	das Wetter	vetter
week	die Woche	vokher
weigh (to)	wiegen	veegen
weight	das Gewicht	ge**veekht**
welcome	willkommen	**vil**commen
well	gut	gōōt
Welsh	walisisch	vuleezish
west	der Westen	vesten
wet	nass	nus
what?	was?	vus
wheel	das Rad	raht
when?	wann?	vun
where?	wo?	voh
whether	ob	op

which?	welcher, e, es?	velkhair, velkher, velkhes
while	während	vairent
who?	wer?	vair
whole	ganz	gunts
whose?	wessen?	vessen
why?	warum?	vahröōm
wide	weit	vîte
widow	die Witwe	veetver
widower	der Witwer	veetvair
wife	die Frau	frow
wild	wild	vilt
win (to)	gewinnen	gevinnen
wind	der Wind	vint
window	das Fenster	fenstair
wing	der Flügel	fluigel
wire	der Draht	draht
wish (to)	wünschen	vuinshen
with	mit	mit
without	ohne	ohner
woman	die Frau	frow
wood	der Wald	valt
wood *timber*	das Holz	holts
wool	die Wolle	voller

word	das Wort	vort
work	die Arbeit	**ar**bite
work (to)	arbeiten	**ar**biten
worry (to)	(sich) beunruhigen	(zikh) beo͞onro͞o-eegen
worse	schlechter	shlekhtair
worth (to be)	wert sein	vairt zine
wrap (to)	wickeln	vickeln
write (to)	schreiben	shriben
writing paper	das Schreibpapier	**shrip**-pupeer
wrong	falsch	fulsh

Y

yacht	die Jacht	yukht
year	das Jahr	yahr
yet	noch	nokh
you	Sie/du (familiar)	zee/do͞o
young	jung	yŏong
your	Ihr, dein	eer, dine
youth hostel	die Jugendherberge	**yoo**gent-hair-bairger

Z

| zip | der Reissverschluss | **rice**-fairshlo͞oss |
| zoo | der Zoo | tsoh |

Index